THE BACKYARD

BBQ

BIBLE

THE BACKYARD
BBQ
BIBLE

100+ RECIPES FOR OUTDOOR GRILLING

OSCAR SMITH

Smith
Street
Books

CONTENTS

INTRO

This book is your guide to getting the absolute best out of your grill – whether it's a modest charcoal bucket or a gas-burning beast with all of the bells and whistles – we've got the best recipes to please a crowd.

Here you'll find more than 100 recipes designed for cooking in the great outdoors. We've covered all the bases – chicken, beef, lamb, pork, fish, and seafood, as well as options for vegetarian entrees.

But what's a steak or a leg of lamb without something delicious to go with it? So, in this book you'll also find a huge selection of salads and sides to go with your meaty (or non-meaty) entrees. We haven't forgotten dessert either – you'll also find sweet recipes that work a treat on the grill.

So fire-up and get cooking!

EQUIPMENT

HERE ARE SOME OF THE ESSENTIAL – AND NOT-SO ESSENTIAL (BUT DEFINITELY HANDY TO HAVE) – BITS AND PIECES FOR GETTING THE MOST OUT OF YOUR OUTDOOR GRILL.

LONG-HANDLED METAL TONGS

Your most important tool. Any metal tongs will do, but it's best to avoid light-weight aluminum ones as they will bend out of shape and tend to heat up more easily.

GRILL BRUSH

For cleaning. You want a brush with stiff metal bristles. If you have a griddle look for a brush that has a scraper attached to it as well.

METAL SPATULA

Essential for turning burgers and delicate fish.

MEAT THERMOMETER

The secret to perfectly cooked meat. There are plenty of different types available at prices to suit any budget, but for grilling, I'd definitely recommend a digital thermometer as they give you an instant read.

BASTING BRUSH

For adding all-important flavor during cooking. Brushes with silicone bristles are much easier to clean than the traditional-style ones, and a long handle is preferable to keep your hands from the heat.

METAL SKEWERS

They're reusable, they don't burn, and they don't require soaking. Stainless steel is best, and ensure the skewers are slightly oval or square, as they grip the food better. Just remember that they do get hot!

PIZZA STONE

Once you make a pizza in your grill, you'll never go back. A pizza stone works especially well in a kettle-shaped cooker as the domed top reflects the heat perfectly.

FISH BASKET

Two wire frames connected by a hinge on one side that can be closed over food and then turned and moved easily using the handles. Brilliant for cooking whole fish.

SMOKER BOX

A great way to get that smoky-flavored goodness even when cooking with gas. A simple cast iron or stainless-steel box that you fill with soaked woodchips and place on top of the grill. (It's also simple to create a smoke box using foil.)

CHOOSING THE RIGHT GRILL

THERE ARE TWO MAIN CAMPS WHEN IT COMES TO OUTDOOR GRILLING: GAS OR CHARCOAL. BOTH HAVE THEIR BENEFITS AND DRAWBACKS, SO IT'S IMPORTANT TO KNOW WHICH WILL BEST SUIT YOUR REQUIREMENTS.

CHARCOAL

There is just no substitute for the distinctive smoky flavor you get from cooking over charcoal. Charcoal grills can also reach higher temperatures than gas grills, allowing for direct, searing heat for perfectly charred steaks that stay rare in the middle. That said, charcoal is messy to handle, it requires much more forethought and lighting time (you'll need to light your charcoal 30–45 minutes beforehand) and charcoal is more expensive and less commonly-available than gas canisters (especially if you're using good-quality hardwood charcoal). But if convenience is not your main priority, then charcoal grilling is an extremely rewarding way to go.

GAS

Quick, clean, and easy, the convenience of a gas grill is hard to beat. A gas grill lights instantly with no other materials required (as long as your gas bottle is full) and usually only takes about 10 minutes to heat. Gas grills also hold their temperatures more steadily and are easy to clean. Some say cooking on gas is a less 'authentic' experience, but if you appreciate the ease of getting home from work, lighting up your grill and having dinner cooked in 15 minutes with no fuss, then a gas grill is a fantastic option.

SIZE

It's important to consider your requirements and available space when buying a grill. There's no sense buying an eight-burner behemoth if you've only got a small balcony to put it on, whereas if you're likely to be regularly cooking for crowds (and have the space) you probably want to consider something on the larger scale.

HOOD

It's absolutely worthwhile getting a grill with a hood or lid. It makes for a much more versatile piece of equipment, allowing you to cook low and slow, roast vegetables or larger pieces of meat, and even hot-smoke fish or ribs.

DURABILITY

This doesn't (always) mean you have to spend a fortune, but, especially if your grill is not going to live undercover, make sure it's made from durable materials. Get yourself a cover if the grill is likely to get wet when it rains.

EXTRAS

If you're willing to pay for them, there's a cornucopia of additional features and add-ons available to the outdoor cook. Some are gimmicks, but a few legitimately useful extras you might look out for are:

- **A rotisserie:** wonderful for slow, even cooking, especially whole chickens or a boneless leg of lamb.

- **Warming racks:** useful if you're cooking for a crowd or if you're grilling a variety of meats or vegetables with different cooking times.

- **A light:** speaks for itself, really. Who hasn't had to pull out their phone torch to check if the sausages are done?

- **An internal thermometer:** great if you're planning on roasting or cooking at low temperatures.

- **A wok burner:** definitely something to consider if you don't have a gas stovetop in your kitchen.

LOOKING AFTER YOUR GRILL

THERE'S NO SENSE IN SPENDING GOOD MONEY ON YOUR GRILL TO NOT KEEP IT IN THE BEST CONDITION YOU CAN. IT DOESN'T TAKE MUCH TIME OR EFFORT TO KEEP IT IN GREAT SHAPE FOR THE YEARS OF COOKING TO COME.

TIPS FOR CLEANING

- **Clean your grill after every use:** grills are much easier to clean when warm, so, once you're done eating, turn the heat back on for a few minutes. Turn the burners off and give the griddle and grill a good scrape with a metal brush to dislodge any food or grease. If there's an excess of grease, use paper towel or newspaper to soak it up.

- **Avoid harsh chemicals:** after all – your food is going on there! Edible acids like lemon juice and vinegar are great for cutting grease. Fill a spray bottle with a 1:1 mixture of water and white vinegar and keep it handy for cleaning.

- **Don't forget the outside of the grill:** absorbent wipes (such as grill wipes) are handy to keep the outside of the grill looking as good as the inside. Remember – looking after your grill now will reward you with many more years of cooking.

MAINTENANCE

- **Do a deep-clean:** every month or two, take the grates and/or griddle out, soak in hot soapy water and give everything a good scrub. You should wear dishwashing gloves when doing this as it will allow you to use hotter water, which helps to cut through grease.

- **Routinely check for gas leaks:** with the gas turned on, run a little soapy water along the gas line and connections. If the water bubbles, there's a leak, and you need to either tighten the connection or replace the line.

- **Keep it covered:** it's well worth getting a cover, especially if your grill is exposed to the elements, including excessive sunshine and rain.

- **Replace the fat absorber pellets regularly:** if you have a drip tray, line it with aluminum foil and fill it with fat absorber pellets (you'll find these at specialist grill stores). These collect the fat drippings from the grill plates, reduce odour, and prevent fat fires from occurring.

HOW TO TELL WHEN YOUR MEAT IS COOKED

THE BEST WAY TO ENSURE PERFECTLY COOKED MEAT EVERY TIME IS TO USE A MEAT THERMOMETER. IF YOU'RE RESTING MEAT BEFORE SERVING (WHICH IS DEFINITELY RECOMMENDED), REMEMBER THAT THE INTERNAL TEMPERATURE WILL RISE DURING THAT TIME, SO REMOVE THE MEAT FROM THE HEAT A LITTLE BIT BEFORE IT REACHES YOUR DESIRED TEMPERATURE.

CHICKEN

Chicken needs to be completely cooked through and never eaten rare. Chicken is cooked when the internal temperature reaches 165°F. When cooking a whole bird, a meat thermometer should be inserted into the thickest part of the thigh. If you don't have a meat thermometer, pierce the same part of the thigh with a sharp knife – if the juices run clear then the chicken is cooked. If they're pink or red then the chicken needs to be cooked a little longer.

PORK

The recommended safe minimum internal temperature of pork is 145°F (160°F for ground pork), followed by a 3-minute rest. For many years, pork had to be overcooked to be deemed safe for consumption, but stricter health regulations over the past few decades means pork can now be enjoyed at its best: medium, still with a little blush of pink in the middle. If you'd prefer it well done, cook to an internal temperature of 160°F.

LAMB

The safe minimum internal temperature of lamb is 145°F, (160°F for ground lamb) followed by a 3-minute rest, which is medium rare. Some people prefer it eaten rare, especially lean cuts like backstrap or tenderloin. Or, if you prefer your meat to have a little more time on the grill, allow 160°F for medium and 170°F for well done.

BEEF

The safe minimum internal temperature of beef is 145°F (160°F for ground beef), followed by a 3-minute rest. As beef is perfectly delicious eaten raw, ideal internal temperature is entirely up to personal preference (and your desired outcome). For best results you shouldn't go much above 145°F as the meat will start to dry out.

CHICKEN

GRILLED PERI PERI CHICKEN

SERVES 4–6

1 × 3 lb whole chicken, butterflied,
   skin patted dry with paper towel
crusty bread, to serve
Portuguese salad (page 147),
   to serve (optional)

PERI PERI SAUCE

5 long red chilies
5 garlic cloves, unpeeled
1 teaspoon dried oregano
1 teaspoon sweet paprika
1 teaspoon soft brown sugar
⅓ cup olive oil
3 tablespoons cider vinegar
1½ teaspoons salt

To make the sauce, first preheat the oven to 430°F. Place the chilies on a baking tray and roast for 10 minutes. Set aside to cool then roughly chop. Meanwhile, blanch the garlic cloves in boiling water for 30 seconds, then peel and roughly chop. Combine with the chili and the remaining ingredients in a small saucepan over medium heat and simmer for 2–3 minutes. Allow the mixture to cool, then puree in a blender.

Place the chicken on a tray and coat with the peri peri sauce, reserving some sauce for basting. Cover with plastic wrap and refrigerate for at least 1 hour.

Preheat a hooded grill to medium and lightly grease with oil.

Place the chicken skin-side down on the grill and cook, covered, for 7–8 minutes. Turn and cook the other side, basting. Continue to cook with the hood closed, turning and basting occasionally, for a further 30 minutes until cooked through.

Serve with crusty bread and, if you like, a side of Portuguese salad.

BRAZILIAN CACHAÇA CHICKEN SKEWERS

SERVES 4–6

2½ lb boneless, skinless chicken
   thighs, each cut into 3 pieces
bamboo skewers, soaked in
   cold water
baby romaine lettuce leaves, to serve
½ cup cilantro leaves
¼ cup mint leaves
1 lime, cut in half

CACHAÇA MARINADE

3 tablespoons olive oil
¼ cup cachaça (see note)
juice of 1 lime
zest of 2 limes
2 garlic cloves, crushed
1 cup mint leaves, torn
1 long red chili, finely chopped
½ teaspoon paprika
1 teaspoon soft brown sugar
1 teaspoon sea salt flakes

To make the marinade, combine the ingredients in a mixing bowl.

Add the chicken pieces to the marinade, stirring well to coat. Cover the bowl in plastic wrap (or transfer the whole lot to a zip-lock bag) and refrigerate for at least 4 hours or overnight.

Preheat a grill to medium and lightly grease with oil.

Thread the chicken pieces onto the skewers and cook on the grill, turning occasionally, for about 6–8 minutes until cooked through.

Pile the lettuce leaves onto a serving platter and place the skewers on top. Scatter with the cilantro and mint leaves, and squeeze the lime juice over the top.

Note: Cachaça is a popular Brazilian distilled spirit made from sugarcane juice. Locally it may be referred to as 'holy water', 'heart opener' and 'tiger breath'. It is available at large liquor stores. This recipe is best started a day ahead to allow the sensational bold flavors to develop.

GRILLED BUTTERMILK CHICKEN

SERVES 4–6

2 cups buttermilk

4 garlic cloves, crushed

2 teaspoons wholegrain mustard

2 teaspoons hot paprika

1 tablespoon sea salt flakes

1 teaspoon freshly ground black
pepper

2 rosemary sprigs, leaves roughly
chopped

1 × 3 lb whole chicken, cut into
quarters

lemon halves, to serve

green salad and Grilled potato
wedges with lime yogurt
(page 138), to serve (optional)

Combine the buttermilk, garlic, mustard, paprika, salt, pepper, and rosemary in a mixing bowl.

Place the chicken in a large zip-lock bag and pour in the buttermilk mixture. Ensure the chicken pieces are well coated. Refrigerate for at least 8 hours or overnight, turning the bag occasionally to disperse the marinade.

Preheat a hooded grill to medium and lightly grease with oil.

Remove the chicken from the marinade and drain. Place the chicken on the grill skin-side down, cover and cook for 20 minutes, turning once after 10 minutes. Turn again and cook for another 5–10 minutes until the chicken is cooked through.

Serve with lemon halves and, if desired, a simple green salad and Grilled potato wedges.

TENNESSEE BEER CAN CHICKEN

SERVES 4

---

1 × 3 lb whole chicken

1 tablespoon olive oil

1½ cups lager-style wheat beer

Grilled potato wedges with lime
  yogurt (page 138), to serve
  (optional)

SPICE RUB

2 teaspoons sweet paprika

2 teaspoons smoked paprika

2 teaspoons soft brown sugar

1 teaspoon ground cumin

½ teaspoon ground coriander

½ teaspoon garlic powder

1 teaspoon sea salt flakes

Preheat a hooded grill to medium-low and lightly grease with oil.

To make the spice rub, mix the ingredients together in a small bowl.

Coat the chicken in the olive oil, and season well with the spice rub mix.

Open the beer can and pour out about a third of the beer. Place the cavity of the chicken over the can, legs down, so that the chicken sits upright. Place carefully on the grill, close the lid and cook for about 1½ hours, until the chicken is cooked through. The chicken is done when a meat thermometer placed into the thickest part of the thigh reads 165°F at minimum, or the juices run clear when pierced with a skewer.

Remove the chicken carefully from the grill and set aside to rest for 20 minutes before removing the can and carving. For a great match, serve with Grilled potato wedges.

APPLE CIDER CHICKEN DRUMSTICKS

SERVES 4

8 chicken drumsticks
1 long red chili, thinly sliced
½ cup mint leaves

APPLE CIDER MARINADE

1 cup apple cider
3 tablespoon peanut oil
3 tablespoons light soy sauce
2 garlic cloves, crushed
¾ in piece ginger, grated
1 fresh red chili, finely chopped
zest of 1 lemon
¼ teaspoon white pepper

To make the marinade, combine the ingredients in a medium-sized bowl.

Place the drumsticks in a large zip-lock bag. Pour in the marinade and seal, pressing out any excess air. Massage to ensure the chicken is well coated with the marinade, and refrigerate for 4 hours, turning occasionally to evenly distribute the marinade.

Remove the chicken from the fridge 30 minutes before cooking to allow it to come to room temperature.

Preheat a grill to medium and lightly grease with oil.

Place the chicken on the grill, cover and cook, turning regularly, for 15 minutes or until cooked through and the juices run clear when the meatiest part of the drumstick is pierced with a skewer.

Serve on a platter garnished with the sliced chili and mint leaves.

GRILLED CHICKEN BURGERS WITH BASIL AIOLI

SERVES 4

4 round wholemeal buns, halved
1 avocado, mashed
1 cup arugula leaves
1 large tomato, sliced

CHICKEN BURGERS

1 lb 2 oz ground chicken
1 garlic clove, finely chopped
¼ cup basil leaves, torn
½ cup flat-leaf parsley leaves, finely chopped
1 teaspoon dried chili flakes
1 teaspoon sea salt flakes
½ teaspoon freshly ground black pepper
zest and juice of 1 lemon
3 tablespoons dry breadcrumbs
1 egg, lightly beaten

BASIL AIOLI

2 egg yolks, at room temperature
2 garlic cloves, finely chopped
½ teaspoon sea salt flakes
3 tablespoons lemon juice
½ cup basil leaves, roughly chopped
¾ cup mild-flavored olive oil

To make the burgers, combine the ingredients in a large mixing bowl. Mix well using your hands until you can see the herbs are evenly dispersed. Using wet hands, shape the mixture into patties slightly larger than the round of the buns. Place the patties on a plate lined with baking paper and cover with plastic wrap. Refrigerate for 1 hour.

To make the aioli, place the egg yolks, garlic, salt, lemon juice, and basil in a food processor and pulse until well combined and creamy. With the motor running, add the oil in a thin, steady stream and keep processing until the mixture thickens. Taste and adjust the seasoning. Refrigerate until needed.

Preheat a griddle to medium and lightly grease with oil.

Cook the burgers for about 4–5 minutes on each side until cooked through. Place the buns, cut-side down, on the griddle to lightly toast. Allow the buns to cool slightly before spreading avocado on the base of each bun, then top with arugula, a chicken burger, and a slice of tomato. Dollop the aioli generously on the tomato then top with the remaining bun halves.

Note: The basil aioli recipe makes about 1 cup. Any remaining aioli can be used on burgers or as a dip for wedges or crudites. It will keep in an airtight container in the fridge for up to 1 week.

FIERY LEMONGRASS CHICKEN WINGS

SERVES 4

2½ lb chicken wings
¼ cup cilantro leaves
1 bird's eye chili, finely sliced

LEMONGRASS MARINADE

2 lemongrass stalks, white part only,
   finely chopped
2 bird's eye chilies, finely sliced
4 cilantro roots and stems, washed
   and finely chopped
4 garlic cloves, finely chopped
3 tablespoons soft brown sugar
1 teaspoon ground turmeric
3 tablespoons peanut oil
juice of 2 limes
3 tablespoons soy sauce
¼ cup fish sauce

To make the marinade, pound the lemongrass, chili, cilantro, and garlic to a paste using a mortar and pestle. Add the sugar and turmeric and mix well. Add the peanut oil, lime juice, and sauces, and stir to combine.

Transfer the marinade to a dish that will comfortably fit the chicken wings. Add the chicken and coat well. Cover with plastic wrap and refrigerate for at least 2 hours, or overnight.

Preheat a hooded grill to medium–low and lightly grease with oil.

Place the chicken wings on the grill and cover with the hood. Cook, turning occasionally, for 25–30 minutes until the marinade has caramelized and charred and the chicken is cooked through.

Pile the wings onto a platter and garnish with the cilantro leaves and sliced chili.

BUTTERFLIED CHICKEN WITH ROSEMARY OIL

SERVES 4–6

1 × 3½ lb whole chicken, butterflied, skin patted dry with paper towel
2 lemons, halved

ROSEMARY OIL

¼ cup rosemary leaves, finely chopped
zest of 1 lemon
2 garlic cloves, roughly chopped
¼ teaspoon freshly ground black pepper
¾ teaspoon sea salt flakes
3 tablespoons olive oil

To make the rosemary oil, pound the rosemary, lemon zest, garlic, pepper, and salt to a paste using a mortar and pestle. Add the oil and mix well.

Rub the rosemary oil all over the chicken, coating the skin and underside well. Reserve a tablespoon of the oil for basting.

Cover the chicken with plastic wrap and set aside for 30 minutes to bring it to room temperature.

Preheat a hooded grill to medium–high and lightly grease with oil.

Place the chicken skin-side down on the grill, cover and reduce the heat to low. Cook for 20 minutes, baste the underside with a sprig of rosemary or a basting brush, then turn the chicken over and baste the skin side. Cover and cook for a further 20 minutes.

If the skin requires further browning and crisping, baste the skin side again and turn over to cook until browned.

Remove from the heat, cover loosely with foil and rest for 10 minutes before carving. Serve with the lemon halves for squeezing over.

BUFFALO WINGS WITH BLUE CHEESE DIP

SERVES 4

½ cup all-purpose flour
½ teaspoon cayenne pepper
½ teaspoon garlic powder
½ teaspoon salt
2½ lb chicken wings
½ cup melted butter
½ cup hot sauce (such as Crystal or Tabasco)

BLUE CHEESE DIP

5½ oz blue cheese
1 cup sour cream
juice of ½ lemon
1 tablespoon white vinegar
salt and freshly ground black pepper

Combine the flour, cayenne pepper, garlic powder, and salt in a dish that will comfortably fit the chicken wings. Add the chicken and toss to coat well. Cover with plastic wrap and refrigerate for at least 1 hour.

Preheat a hooded grill to medium–low and lightly grease with oil.

Whisk together the melted butter and hot sauce. Dip the wings into the butter mixture, and place on a tray.

Place the chicken wings on the grill and cover with the hood. Cook, turning occasionally, for 25–30 minutes until the outside has caramelized a little and the chicken is cooked through.

Meanwhile, to make the blue cheese dip, mash the cheese to a paste using a fork then combine with the other ingredients in a small bowl. Taste and season with salt and pepper.

Pile the wings onto a platter and serve with the dip alongside.

LEMON& GARLIC CHICKEN WINGS

SERVES 4

1 tablespoon olive oil

4 garlic cloves, crushed

7 fl oz lemon juice

2½ lb chicken wings

1 lemon, finely sliced

1 small handful cilantro leaves, finely
  chopped

1 teaspoon nigella seeds

Greek-style yogurt, thinned with a
  little water, to serve

Combine the olive oil, garlic, and lemon juice in a dish that will comfortably fit the chicken wings and season generously with salt and pepper. Add the wings and lemon slices and mix to coat well. Cover and refrigerate for at least 2 hours or overnight.

Preheat a hooded grill to medium–low and lightly grease with oil.

Place the chicken wings on the grill and cover with the hood. Cook, turning occasionally, for 25–30 minutes until the outside has caramelized a little and the chicken is cooked through.

Pile the wings onto a platter, sprinkle with the cilantro and nigella seeds, and drizzle with a little yogurt.

SPICY SATAY CHICKEN SKEWERS

SERVES 4

1 lb 5 oz boneless, skinless chicken thighs, cut evenly into 1¼ inch strips

bamboo skewers, soaked in cold water

iceberg lettuce leaves, to serve

cucumber slices, to serve

½ fresh pineapple, cut into chunks

MARINADE

2 lemongrass stalks, white part only, thinly sliced

2 garlic cloves, roughly chopped

2 teaspoons finely grated palm sugar

1 teaspoon ground coriander

1 teaspoon ground cumin

1 teaspoon ground turmeric

1 tablespoon peanut oil

PEANUT SAUCE

1¼ cups raw unsalted peanuts

12 dried red chilies, deseeded

2 lemongrass stalks, white part only, finely chopped

3 shallots, finely chopped

2 garlic cloves, finely chopped

1 tablespoon ground coriander

2 teaspoons finely grated palm sugar

¼ cup peanut oil

1 tablespoon tamarind paste

1 tablespoon kecap manis

½ cup coconut milk

To make the marinade, pound the lemongrass and garlic into a paste using a mortar and pestle. Add the palm sugar, coriander, cumin, turmeric, and oil, and mix well.

Transfer the marinade to a bowl, add the chicken and mix well. Cover with plastic wrap and refrigerate for at least 4 hours or overnight.

To make the sauce, first preheat the oven to 350°F. Spread the peanuts on a baking tray and roast for about 5 minutes until fragrant and lightly golden. Set aside to cool, then finely chop. Meanwhile, soak the chilies in hot water for 15 minutes. Drain and roughly chop. Place the chili into a food processor along with the lemongrass, shallots, garlic, coriander, sugar, and peanut oil and process until a paste forms. Heat a medium-sized saucepan over medium heat and add the chili paste. Cook, stirring continuously for 5 minutes. Add 2 cups water and bring to the boil, then add the tamarind, kecap manis, peanuts, and coconut milk. Simmer for 5 minutes over low heat or until thickened.

Preheat a grill to medium–high and lightly grease with oil.

Thread 3-4 chicken pieces onto each skewer so that the chicken lies fairly flat. Cook on the grill, turning regularly, for 3-4 minutes until slightly charred and cooked through. (Cooking time will be determined by the thickness of the chicken.)

Arrange the lettuce, cucumber, pineapple, and skewers onto plates. Serve with a small bowl of sauce for each person.

CHIPOTLE CHICKEN BURRITOS

SERVES 4

1 lb 2 oz chicken tenderloins, trimmed

2 corn cobs

4 burrito tortillas

14 oz tinned black beans, rinsed and drained

½ iceberg lettuce, shredded

½ cup cilantro leaves

CHIPOTLE MARINADE

1 tablespoon chipotle chilies in adobo sauce, chopped

3 tablespoons honey

3 garlic cloves, crushed

2 teaspoons sea salt

FRESH TOMATO SALSA

3 ripe tomatoes, diced

½ red onion, finely diced

1 jalapeño chili, finely chopped

¼ cup cilantro leaves, chopped

1 avocado, diced

½ teaspoon salt

juice of ½ lime

CHIPOTLE AIOLI

2 egg yolks, at room temperature

¼ teaspoon sea salt flakes

juice of ½ lemon

1 small garlic clove, crushed

3 tablespoons chipotle chilies in adobo sauce, chopped

1 cup mild-flavored olive oil

To make the marinade, combine the ingredients in a medium-sized bowl. Add the chicken, and mix to coat well. Cover with plastic wrap and refrigerate for 1 hour.

To make the salsa, combine the tomato, onion, chili, cilantro, and avocado in a medium-sized bowl. Add the salt and lime juice and mix well.

To make the aioli, place the egg yolks, salt, lemon juice, garlic, and chipotle chili into a small food processor. Process on low and add the oil in a thin, steady stream until incorporated.

Preheat a grill to high and lightly grease with oil.

Grill the corn, turning occasionally, for about 8–10 minutes until well blackened all over. Remove and set aside to cool. Remove the kernels from the cobs using a sharp knife.

Reduce the grill heat to medium. Cook the chicken for about 10 minutes or until cooked through, turning every 3 minutes. The honey will make the chicken more likely to burn, so frequent turning is important.

To assemble the burritos, first warm the tortillas for 5–10 seconds on the grill. Top each burrito with chicken, salsa, corn, beans, lettuce, and cilantro, and then drizzle with the chipotle aioli. (The key to wrapping a burrito is to not overfill, so make sure no more than a third of the tortilla is covered.) Fold in both sides, and then roll the tortilla to contain the filling.

Note: The aioli recipe makes about 1½ cups. Any remaining aioli can be used on burgers or as a dip for the Grilled potato wedges on page 138. It will keep in an airtight container in the fridge for up to 1 week.

PORK

PORK TENDERLOIN WITH MAPLE, GINGER & ORANGE GLAZE

SERVES 4

zest and juice of 2 oranges

⅓ cup apple cider vinegar

2 in piece ginger, peeled and finely grated

2 teaspoons dijon mustard

1½ teaspoons smoked paprika

1½ teaspoons sea salt flakes

1 tablespoon olive oil

2–3 pork tenderloins (about 1½ lb in total)

½ cup pure maple syrup

Chargrilled Belgian endive (page 143), to serve (optional)

In a small saucepan, combine the orange zest and juice, vinegar, ginger, mustard, paprika, and salt. Simmer over medium–low heat for 3–4 minutes. Set aside to cool.

Transfer ¼ cup of the marinade to a large zip-lock bag along with the oil. Add the pork and seal, pushing out as much of the air as you can. Massage the marinade into the pork and place in the fridge for at least 1 hour.

Meanwhile, add the maple syrup to the remaining marinade in the saucepan to make the glaze. Simmer for 4–5 minutes until reduced and thickened slightly. Reserve half the glaze for serving.

Preheat a grill to medium–high and lightly grease with oil.

Cook the pork for 2 minutes each side until browned all over. Reduce the heat to medium–low and cook, turning and basting with the glaze, for a further 10–12 minutes or until cooked through.

Cover the pork and rest for 5 minutes.

Cut the pork into ½ in slices and spoon the reserved glaze over the top. If desired, serve with Chargrilled Belgian endive.

ASPARAGUS WRAPPED IN BACON

SERVES 4

2 bunches asparagus, ends trimmed
4 slices rindless streaky bacon
olive oil, for drizzling
1 tablespoon brown sugar
1 tablespoon toasted black sesame
  seeds

Preheat a grill to medium.

Divide the asparagus into four bundles. Wrap each bundle with a slice of bacon and secure with a piece of kitchen string. Drizzle with a little olive oil.

Cook the asparagus, turning carefully every now and then, for 6–8 minutes until the asparagus is lightly charred and the bacon is cooked through. Sprinkle all over with sugar and cook for a further 1–2 minutes until the sugar is caramelized.

Serve immediately scattered liberally with the sesame seeds and seasoned with pepper.

CHERRY TOMATO & BACON SKEWERS

SERVES 4

9 oz cherry tomatoes

9 oz haloumi, cut into cubes

4 bamboo skewers, soaked in warm
water for 30 minutes

4 slices rindless streaky bacon, cut
in half lengthways

Preheat a grill to medium.

Thread the cherry tomatoes and haloumi alternately onto the skewers, weaving the bacon on the skewer between the pieces. You will need two strips of bacon per skewer. If there is bacon left over at the end of each skewer, just keep threading it on.

Cook the skewers, turning carefully every now and then for 8–10 minutes until the haloumi is lightly charred and the bacon is cooked through. It's important not to have the barbecue or chargrill too hot as the bacon needs a chance to cook through before the tomatoes and cheese.

Season with a little salt and pepper to serve.

HOMEMADE PORK & FENNEL SAUSAGES

MAKES 2 LB

2 tablespoons fennel seeds

2 lb ground pork, at least 30% fat content (see note)

1 tablespoon freshly ground black pepper

1 tablespoon salt

2 teaspoons dried chili flakes (optional)

¼ cup chilled dry white wine

natural sausage casings (see note)

Note: You can ask your butcher to grind your choice of cut for sausages – scotch fillet, shoulder, and belly pork are all ideal. A fairly coarse grind and a minimum of 30% fat will give you the best result.

Note: Sausage casings can be ordered through your local butcher. Natural casings are best. Casings are stored salted so must be rinsed inside and out with cold water before use.

Toast the fennel seeds in a small dry frying pan over medium heat until fragrant. Transfer to a large mixing bowl and add the pork, pepper, salt, and chili flakes (if using). Using your hands, mix well until the mixture becomes sticky. (This is an important step as it will improve the final texture.) Add the wine and continue to mix.

The flavoring can be checked at this stage by cooking a spoonful of pork mixture in a small frying pan with a little olive oil over medium–high heat. Taste and adjust the seasoning if necessary.

Run cold tap water through the sausage casings until the water runs clean. Cut a length of casing about 6½ ft long and feed the casing onto the nozzle of a sausage maker. Leave a bit of casing hanging over to allow any excess air to escape. Feed the pork mixture through the machine or nozzle, assisting the casing to slide off the nozzle as it is filled. Press out any air bubbles. Tie the end in a knot, and working towards the untied end, twist the filled casing into sausage lengths. Tie the open end in a knot. (If you don't have a sausage maker you can make the sausages by hand using a wide-necked funnel.)

Place the sausages onto a plate and cover with a clean dish towel. Refrigerate overnight or for up to 48 hours before cooking (this allows the flavors to develop and also reduces the likelihood of the skins splitting).

Preheat a grill to medium and lightly grease with oil.

Cook the sausages, turning occasionally for about 10 minutes until cooked through.

HOMEMADE PORK & VEAL SAUSAGES

MAKES ABOUT 5½ LB

3 lb ground pork, at least 30% fat content (see note on page opposite), chilled

2 lb 3 oz ground veal, chilled

½ cup finely chopped flat-leaf parsley

½ cup powdered milk

3 tablespoons salt

1 tablespoon finely grated lemon zest

2 teaspoons ground white pepper

2 teaspoons ground mustard seeds

1 teaspoon ground celery seeds

1 teaspoon onion powder

natural pork sausage casings (see note on page opposite)

Place the pork and veal in a chilled mixing bowl and add the parsley, powdered milk, salt, lemon zest, white pepper, mustard seeds, celery seeds, and onion powder. Using your hands, mix well until the mixture becomes sticky. (This is an important step as it will improve the final texture.)

The flavoring can be checked at this stage by cooking a spoonful of pork mixture in a small frying pan with a little olive oil over medium–high heat. Taste and adjust the seasoning if necessary.

Run cold tap water through the sausage casings until the water runs clean. Cut a length of casing about 6½ ft long and feed the casing onto the nozzle of a sausage maker. Leave a bit of casing hanging over to allow any excess air to escape. Feed the pork mixture through the machine or nozzle, assisting the casing to slide off the nozzle as it is filled. Press out any air bubbles. Tie the end in a knot, and working towards the untied end, twist the filled casing into sausage lengths. Tie the open end in a knot. (If you don't have a sausage maker you can make the sausages by hand using a wide-necked funnel.)

Place the sausages onto a plate and cover with a clean dish towel. Refrigerate overnight or for up to 48 hours before cooking (this allows the flavors to develop and also reduces the likelihood of the skins splitting).

Preheat a grill to medium and lightly grease with oil.

Cook the sausages, turning occasionally for about 10 minutes until cooked through.

GRILLED PORK RIBS WITH VIETNAMESE DIPPING SAUCE

SERVES 4

3½ lb pork spare or baby back rib
  racks, cut into individual ribs
iceberg lettuce leaves, to serve
mint sprigs, to serve
cilantro sprigs, to serve
cucumber cut into sticks, to serve
small red chilies, sliced, to serve

MARINADE

4 shallots, sliced
4 scallions, roughly chopped
1 lemongrass stalk, white part only,
  chopped
1 cup coarsely chopped cilantro
  stems, roots and leaves
2 in piece ginger, peeled and sliced
6 garlic cloves, peeled
⅓ cup fish sauce
3 tablespoons soy sauce
1 tablespoon rice vinegar
3 tablespoons finely grated palm
  sugar
1 teaspoon ground white pepper

DIPPING SAUCE

¼ cup fish sauce
3 tablespoons rice vinegar
3 tablespoons superfine sugar
2 garlic cloves, finely chopped
1 small red chili, finely sliced
3 tablespoons lime juice

To make the marinade, place the ingredients in a food processor and process until finely chopped.

Place the pork ribs in a large bowl and coat well with the marinade. Cover with plastic wrap and refrigerate for up to 5 hours, tossing occasionally.

Preheat a hooded grill to medium–low and lightly grease with oil.

Place the ribs bone-side down on the grill, reserving the marinade for basting. Cover and cook, basting with the marinade every 15 minutes, for 1 hour. Turn the ribs, baste and reduce the heat to low. Cover and cook for a further 30 minutes until tender.

Meanwhile, to make the dipping sauce, combine the fish sauce, vinegar, and sugar with ⅓ cup water in a small saucepan over medium heat. Bring to just below boiling point then set aside to cool. Add the garlic, chili, and lime juice, and stir to combine.

Transfer the ribs to a serving platter and arrange the lettuce, mint, cilantro, cucumber, and chili around them. Serve the dipping sauce in small bowls.

HOMEMADE
BRATWURST

MAKES 7 LB 12 OZ

5½ lb ground pork , at least 30% fat
content (see note page 44), chilled
2 lb ground veal, chilled
2 oz salt
1 tablespoon dried marjoram
1½ teaspoons ground white pepper
1 teaspoon mustard powder
1 teaspoon ground allspice
1 teaspoon onion powder
¼ teaspoon ground ginger
natural pork sausage casings
(see note page 44)
crusty white rolls, to serve
wholegrain mustard, to serve

Place the pork and veal in a chilled mixing bowl and add the salt, marjoram, white pepper, mustard powder, allspice, onion powder, and ginger. Using your hands, mix well until the mixture becomes sticky. (This is an important step as it will improve the final texture.)

The flavoring can be checked at this stage by cooking a spoonful of pork mixture in a small frying pan with a little olive oil over medium–high heat. Taste and adjust the seasoning if necessary.

Run cold tap water through the sausage casings until the water runs clean. Cut a length of casing about 6½ ft long and feed the casing onto the nozzle of a sausage maker. Leave a bit of casing hanging over to allow any excess air to escape. Feed the pork mixture through the machine or nozzle, assisting the casing to slide off the nozzle as it is filled. Press out any air bubbles. Tie the end in a knot, and working towards the untied end, twist the filled casing into sausage lengths. Tie the open end in a knot. (If you don't have a sausage maker you can make the sausages by hand using a wide-necked funnel.)

Place the sausages onto a plate and cover with a clean dish towel. Refrigerate overnight or for up to 48 hours before cooking (this allows the flavors to develop and also reduces the likelihood of the skins splitting).

Preheat a grill to medium and lightly grease with oil.

Cook the sausages, turning occasionally for about 10 minutes until cooked through.

Serve in crusty white rolls spread with wholegrain mustard.

CURRYWURST SERVES 4

4 Bratwurst sausages (see recipe
on page opposite)

CURRY SAUCE

1 tablespoon vegetable oil
1 small white onion, finely chopped
1 garlic clove, crushed
1 tablespoon mild curry powder
2¼ cups tomato puree
⅓ cup white wine vinegar
⅓ cup sugar
2 teaspoons worcestershire sauce
2 teaspoons salt
2 teaspoons sweet paprika
1 teaspoon mustard powder

To make the curry sauce, heat the oil in a saucepan over medium-low heat and add the onion. Cook for 3-4 minutes until soft and translucent. Add the garlic and cook for a further 2 minutes, making sure the garlic doesn't burn. Add the curry powder and cook, stirring, for 1 minute before adding the tomato puree. Heat until simmering, then add the vinegar, sugar, worcestershire sauce, salt, paprika, and mustard powder. Simmer, uncovered, for 15 minutes or until thickened. Remove from the heat and process with a hand-held blender until smooth.

Preheat a grill to high and lightly grease with oil.

Score each sausage to one-quarter of its depth with a sharp knife at ½ in intervals, to indicate bite-sized pieces. Cook the sausages for about 20 minutes until cooked through.

To serve, slice the sausages through the score lines. Transfer to serving plates and spoon the sauce over the top.

SOUTHERN-STYLE BABY BACK PORK RIBS

SERVES 4

3½ lb baby back pork ribs, cut into
    racks of 4 ribs each
Grilled cabbage salad (page 162),
    to serve (optional)

DRY RUB

3 tablespoons sea salt flakes
2 tablespoons sweet paprika
2 teaspoons smoked paprika
2 teaspoons garlic powder
1 teaspoon dried oregano
1 teaspoon celery salt
1 teaspoon chili flakes

BARBECUE SAUCE

½ red onion, finely chopped
2 garlic cloves, finely chopped
3 tablespoons soft brown sugar
1 teaspoon sweet paprika
½ teaspoon smoked paprika
½ cup tomato ketchup
¼ cup cider vinegar
¼ cup pure maple syrup

Preheat a hooded grill to low.

To make the dry rub, combine the ingredients in a small bowl.

Coat the ribs in the dry rub, then wrap in foil. Place 2–3 racks in each foil package for easy handling.

Place the foil packs on the grill and cover. Cook for 2 hours, turning every 30 minutes.

Meanwhile, to make the barbecue sauce, combine the ingredients in a small saucepan with 1 cup water. Cook over low heat for 20–25 minutes until thick. Reserve half the sauce for serving.

Remove the foil packages from the grill. Increase the heat to medium and lightly grease with oil. Carefully unwrap the ribs and discard the foil. Brush the ribs all over with the barbecue sauce and return to the grill. Cook, basting and turning regularly, for 30 minutes, or until the ribs are browned and sticky, caramelized and charred.

Pile the ribs onto a serving platter and serve with the reserved barbecue sauce and, if desired, Grilled cabbage salad.

BACON-WEAVE CHEESEBURGERS

SERVES 4

1½ lb ground beef

2 onions: 1 grated; 1 thinly sliced

1 teaspoon dijon mustard

1 large egg, beaten

½ cup fresh breadcrumbs

⅓ cup finely grated parmesan

12 slices rindless streaky bacon

4 soft burger buns, halved

4 slices Swiss cheese

mayonnaise, sliced dill pickles,
   shredded lettuce, and thinly sliced
   tomato, to serve

Preheat the oven to 350°F. Line a baking tray with foil, folding up the edges of the foil to contain the rendered bacon fat.

Combine the beef, grated onion, mustard, egg, breadcrumbs, and parmesan in a bowl. Season with salt and pepper, mix with damp hands, and then form into four patties. Chill for 30 minutes.

Meanwhile, make a weave or lattice with the bacon strips to form a square on the prepared tray. Place an upturned wire rack over the bacon to keep it flat while it cooks. Cook the bacon for 25–30 minutes until browned and crisp. Remove from the oven, carefully remove the rack and place the bacon weave on paper towel. Cut into four even squares. Reserve the rendered fat from the bacon tray. Turn off the oven, place the bacon squares on the tray and return to the oven to keep warm.

Preheat a griddle to high and lightly grease with oil.

Brush the cut side of each of the buns with the reserved bacon fat. Set aside.

Place the patties on the griddle, flatten slightly and cook for 8–10 minutes until well crusted and browned, turning occasionally. Top the patties with the cheese slices and cook for a minute or so more until the cheese starts to melt and the patties are just cooked through. Transfer to a plate.

Meanwhile, add the sliced onion to the griddle and cook, stirring often, for 4–5 minutes until tender and browned. Pile on top of the cheese on the patties.

Grill the cut side of the burger buns until golden. Spread mayonnaise on the toasted side of each bun. Place a few slices of pickle on each bottom bun. Top with lettuce, tomato, a patty, and a square of bacon weave. Close the buns and serve immediately.

BACON-WRAPPED MAC & CHEESE BURGERS MAKES 6

1⅔ cups macaroni

3 tablespoons butter

2 shallots, finely chopped

2 tablespoons all-purpose flour, plus extra for coating

1 cup full-cream milk

1 cup grated gruyère or smoked cheddar

¾ cup finely grated parmesan

2 large eggs, lightly beaten

1⅓ cups panko (Japanese breadcrumbs)

½ cup sunflower or vegetable oil

6 slices rindless bacon

6 burger or brioche buns, halved and toasted

dijonnaise or smoky tomato ketchup, shredded lettuce, and thinly sliced tomato, to serve

Line a 13 in x 9 in baking tray with baking paper. Bring a large saucepan of salted water to the boil. Cook the macaroni according to the packet directions or until al dente, stirring often to prevent sticking. Drain.

Meanwhile, melt the butter in a saucepan. Add the shallots and cook for 3–4 minutes until soft. Stir in the flour. Remove from the heat and slowly stir in the milk. Return to the heat and gently bring to the boil, stirring until thickened. Remove from the heat and stir in the cheeses until melted. Season with salt and pepper then stir in the macaroni until well combined. Pour into the prepared tray, pressing down with a wooden spoon to compact the macaroni mixture. Refrigerate for at least 3 hours to set.

Preheat a grill to high and lightly grease with oil.

Turn the macaroni out onto a clean work surface and cut into six rounds using a 3½ in cutter. (Save any leftover mac and cheese and reheat as a snack.)

Place the extra flour, egg, and breadcrumbs, into three separate shallow bowls. Coat each macaroni patty in the flour, shaking off the excess, followed by the beaten egg, then into the breadcrumbs, pressing on to coat well. Place onto a plate.

Heat the oil in a large non-stick frying pan until very hot. Shallow-fry the patties, three at a time, for 2–3 minutes on each side until golden. Transfer to a plate lined with paper towel to drain.

Wrap a slice of bacon the whole way around each patty and secure the ends with a toothpick. Butter the cut sides of the buns. Cook the bacon-wrapped patties on the grill for 3–4 minutes on each side, until the bacon is golden. Remove the toothpicks. Grill the cut sides of the buns.

Serve the patties on the toasted buns spread with dijonnaise, topped with lettuce and tomato.

SMOKY CHIPOTLE GRILLED PORK RIBS

SERVES 4

4 racks baby back pork ribs, each cut in half

DRY RUB

1 tablespoon sea salt flakes

1 tablespoon smoked paprika

2 teaspoons soft brown sugar

2 teaspoons dried oregano

1½ teaspoons freshly ground black pepper

SAUCE

1 tablespoon olive oil

2 garlic cloves, crushed

2 cooking apples, peeled, cored, and grated

1 teaspoon sea salt

1 teaspoon sweet paprika

2 chipotle chilies in adobo sauce, chopped

1 cup pureed tomatoes

¼ cup maple syrup

3 tablespoons cider vinegar

Preheat the oven to 300°F.

Combine the dry rub ingredients in a small bowl. Sprinkle evenly over both sides of the pork ribs, pressing it in well. Wrap the ribs in foil, then place in a single layer on a large baking tray. Transfer to the oven and bake for 2½ hours. Remove the foil-wrapped ribs from the oven and leave until cool enough to handle.

To make the sauce, heat the olive oil in a small saucepan over low heat and cook the garlic and apple for about 4 minutes until soft. Stir in the salt, paprika, chilies, pureed tomatoes, maple syrup, and vinegar. Continue to cook over low heat, stirring occasionally, for about 10 minutes, until the mixture is thick and saucy. Set aside.

Preheat a grill to medium heat.

Unwrap the ribs, and brush the sauce over both sides. Grill the ribs on both sides, until charred. Transfer the ribs to a chopping board. Use a sharp knife to cut between the bones.

Pile the ribs onto a platter to serve.

JAMAICAN JERK PORK BELLY

SERVES 8

3½ lb pork belly
Apple & cabbage slaw (page 142),
  to serve (optional)

JERK MARINADE

6 scallions, roughly chopped
2 garlic cloves, roughly chopped
3 scotch bonnet chilies, deseeded
  (if you prefer less heat) and sliced
¾ in piece ginger, peeled and grated
3 tablespoons soft brown sugar
3 tablespoons fresh thyme leaves
3 tablespoons ground allspice
1 tablespoon sea salt flakes
2 teaspoons ground nutmeg
2 teaspoons ground cinnamon
2 bay leaves, torn
½ cup olive oil
¼ cup soy sauce
juice of 1 lime
zest and juice of 1 orange
½ cup cider vinegar

To make the marinade, place the ingredients in a food processor and blend until smooth.

Place the pork in a baking dish. Pour the marinade over and massage into the pork. Cover with plastic wrap and refrigerate for at least 2 hours, or overnight.

Preheat a grill to medium–high and lightly grease with oil.

Place the pork on the grill, reserving the excess marinade for basting. Cook for 10–15 minutes on each side, then reduce the heat to low. Continue to cook, basting and turning every 20 minutes for 1½ hours, or until dark and tender.

Remove from the heat, cover and rest for 15 minutes before slicing.

KOREAN GRILLED PORK

SERVES 6

2½ lb pork belly, cut into 3 in pieces,
   then very thinly sliced
oakleaf lettuce leaves, to serve
scallions, cut into 4 in lengths, to
   serve
green chilies, sliced, to serve
toasted sesame seeds, to serve

MARINADE

½ onion, sliced
½ cup grated nashi pear
3 scallions, finely chopped
4 garlic cloves, crushed
½ teaspoon grated ginger
¼ cup gochujang (Korean red
   pepper paste)
¼ cup soft brown sugar
3 tablespoons rice cooking wine
1 tablespoon soy sauce
2 teaspoons sesame oil
1 tablespoon sesame seeds
3 tablespoons fish sauce

To make the marinade, combine the ingredients in a large bowl. Season with pepper. Add the pork and mix to coat well. Cover with plastic wrap and refrigerate for at least 2 hours.

Heat a griddle to high and lightly grease with oil.

Cook the pork in batches. Place pieces of pork on the griddle in a single layer (avoid crowding). Cook for 2 minutes on each side or until caramelized. Transfer to a serving plate and keep warm while the remaining pork is cooked.

Arrange the lettuce leaves, scallions, and chilies on the serving plate around the pork. Sprinkle with the sesame seeds and serve.

SEAFOOD

SPICED FISH TACOS WITH CHIPOTLE SAUCE

SERVES 4–6

2½ lb skinless firm white fish (such as cod or tilapia), cut into 4 in x 1¼ in pieces
olive oil, for brushing
2 cups cilantro leaves, roughly chopped
1 white onion, very finely chopped
12 corn tortillas
¼ green cabbage, finely shredded
6 radishes, thinly shaved
3 limes, cut into wedges

CHIPOTLE SAUCE

½ cup whole egg mayonnaise
½ cup Greek-style yogurt
1 small chipotle chili in adobo sauce, finely chopped, plus 1 teaspoon of sauce
½ teaspoon dried oregano
1 tablespoon finely chopped dill
zest and juice of 1 lime

SPICE MIX

1 teaspoon paprika
½ teaspoon ground cumin
½ teaspoon freshly ground black pepper
½ teaspoon dried oregano
½ teaspoon sea salt flakes

To make the sauce, place the ingredients in a blender and blend until smooth. Transfer to a serving bowl and season with salt and pepper to taste. Cover with plastic wrap and refrigerate until needed.

Preheat a griddle to medium–high and lightly grease with oil.

To make the spice mix, combine the ingredients in a small bowl.

Pat the fish dry with paper towel, then brush with olive oil and sprinkle with the spice mix. Cover with plastic wrap and refrigerate for 10 minutes.

Combine the cilantro and onion in a small bowl.

Cook the fish, turning once, for approximately 2 minutes each side until just cooked through.

Toast the tortillas on one side on the griddle or grill for about 30 seconds until lightly charred.

Serve the fish in a pile along with the tortillas, chipotle sauce, cilantro and onion, a pile of the cabbage and radishes, and lime wedges.

LOUISIANA SHRIMP PO'BOY

SERVES 4

1½ lb large raw shrimp, shelled
and deveined

bamboo skewers, soaked in cold
water

1 long baguette, cut into 4 lengths
then halved horizontally

2 cucumbers, sliced into thin lengths

½ green oakleaf lettuce, washed and
drained thoroughly

LOUISIANA MARINADE

3 tablespoons olive oil

1 garlic clove, finely chopped

1 teaspoon sweet paprika

½ teaspoon salt

¼ teaspoon freshly ground
black pepper

¼ teaspoon cayenne pepper

½ teaspoon dried oregano

½ teaspoon dried thyme

REMOULADE

½ cup good-quality whole egg
mayonnaise

1 teaspoon dijon mustard

juice of ½ lemon

2 teaspoons capers, roughly chopped

¼ teaspoon cayenne pepper

¼ teaspoon sweet paprika

To make the marinade, combine the ingredients in a large mixing bowl. Add the shrimp and toss to coat well. Cover and refrigerate for 30 minutes.

To make the remoulade, combine the ingredients in a small mixing bowl. Mix well and set aside.

Heat a grill to medium and lightly grease with oil.

Thread the shrimp onto the bamboo skewers and cook for 2–3 minutes on each side.

Fill the baguettes with cucumber and lettuce. Remove the shrimp from the skewers and pile onto the lettuce. Top with remoulade and serve.

WHOLE SNAPPER WITH THAI FLAVORS SERVES 4

3 long red chilies, deseeded and
coarsely chopped

2 lemongrass stalks, white part only,
thinly sliced

1 tablespoon grated palm sugar

½ bunch cilantro, leaves picked and
stems roughly chopped

1 tablespoon fish sauce

3 tablespoons coconut milk

banana leaves, for wrapping

2½ lb whole snapper, cleaned
and scaled

2 limes, sliced, plus extra lime
wedges to serve

4 kaffir lime leaves, torn

Preheat a grill to medium-high and lightly grease with oil.

Pound the chilies, lemongrass, palm sugar, and cilantro to a coarse paste using a mortar and pestle. Transfer to a small mixing bowl, add the fish sauce and coconut milk and stir to combine.

Lay the banana leaves out on a large board, overlapping to form a piece large enough to wrap the fish.

Make four diagonal, ½ in deep cuts in each side of the snapper. Coat the top of the fish with half the chili paste, working it into the cuts. Place the fish, paste-side down, in the center of the banana leaves. Fill the cavity with lime slices and kaffir lime leaves and spread the chili paste over the fish. Wrap the banana leaves to enclose, then wrap in foil.

Place the parcel on the grill and cook for 8–9 minutes on each side, until just cooked through.

Serve with lime wedges.

GRILLED TUNA WITH GARLIC & CAPER AIOLI

SERVES 4

4 tuna steaks, ¾ in thick
Summer veg ratatouille parcels
  (page 132), to serve (optional)

GARLIC & CAPER AIOLI

2 garlic cloves, crushed
1 teaspoon sea salt flakes
2 egg yolks
1 cup olive oil
1 tablespoon lemon juice
2 tablespoons baby capers, drained
1 tablespoon finely chopped
  flat-leaf parsley

MARINADE

zest of 1 lemon
1 tablespoon sea salt flakes
1 teaspoon coarse ground
  black pepper
¼ cup olive oil

To make the aioli, place the garlic, salt, and egg yolks in a small food processor and blend until well combined. With the motor running, add the oil in a thin, steady stream, until the aioli thickens. Transfer to a small bowl. Stir in the lemon juice, capers, and parsley. Cover and refrigerate until required.

To make the marinade, combine the ingredients in a small bowl. Brush the tuna with the marinade then place in a zip-lock bag and refrigerate for at least 2 hours, or overnight.

Preheat a grill to high and lightly grease with oil.

Allow the tuna to come to room temperature before cooking.

Cook the tuna steaks for about 2 minutes until the red tuna turns beige part of the way up the side. Turn and cook for another 2 minutes, or until the color of the tuna changes as before and you can just see a line of pink from the side.

Serve with a generous dollop of the aioli, and if you like, Summer veg ratatouille parcels to accompany.

FLOUNDER WITH BURNT BUTTER, CAPERS & SAGE

SERVES 4

4 × 1 lb whole flounder, rinsed
   and dried
3 tablespoons olive oil
banana leaves, for wrapping
3½ oz butter
⅓ cup capers, drained
20 sage leaves
lemon cheeks, to serve

Brush each flounder with oil and season with salt.

Place a large sheet of foil onto a clean work surface. Cover with a banana leaf. Place one flounder on the banana leaf, top-side down, and wrap carefully to enclose.

Repeat with the remaining fish.

Preheat a griddle to medium–high and lightly grease with oil.

Cook the flounder for 4–5 minutes, turn and continue cooking for 2–3 minutes until cooked through.

Meanwhile, place a small frying pan on the griddle to heat. Add the butter and swirl in the pan to heat evenly. When it starts to foam, add the capers and sage and cook for 1 minute or until crisp.

Serve each flounder on its banana leaf and spoon the hot butter, capers, and sage over the top, with a lemon cheek alongside.

JAPANESE SEVEN-SPICE CALAMARI

SERVES 4

1 lb 2 oz squid hoods, cleaned
and cut into ¾ in rings, leave
tentacles intact

3 tablespoons sesame seeds,
toasted until golden

2 scallions, thinly sliced
on the diagonal

JAPANESE MARINADE

½ cup light soy sauce

2 in piece of ginger, peeled and
finely grated

¼ cup mirin

1 tablespoon shichimi togarashi
(see note)

1 tablespoon peanut oil

To make the marinade, combine the ingredients in a large bowl. Reserve half the marinade for basting.

Add the squid to the remaining marinade and mix well to coat. Set aside in the fridge to marinate for 15 minutes.

Preheat a grill to high and lightly grease with oil.

Grill the squid, turning frequently and basting with the reserved marinade, for 2–3 minutes until opaque and tender. Take care not to overcook the squid as it can quickly become rubbery.

Serve garnished with the toasted sesame seeds and scallions.

Note: Shichimi togarashi is a traditional Japanese seven-spice mix, predominantly made up of red pepper, and is available from Asian grocery stores.

SUGARCANE SHRIMP

SERVES 4–6

8 garlic cloves, roughly chopped

5 Asian shallots, roughly chopped

4 lemongrass stalks, white part only, finely chopped

3 tablespoons grated palm sugar

3 tablespoons light fish sauce

3½ lb raw shrimp, shelled and deveined

1 egg white

1 tablespoon finely chopped cilantro leaves

white pepper, to taste

4 pieces tinned sugarcane, cut lengthways into ½ in pieces

NUOC CHAM DIPPING SAUCE

3 tablespoons superfine sugar

⅓ cup rice vinegar

⅓ cup fish sauce

¼ cup lime juice

2 garlic cloves, very finely chopped

1 long red chili, finely sliced

Place the garlic, shallots, lemongrass, and palm sugar in a food processor and pulse to a paste. Add the fish sauce, shrimp, and egg white and process until smooth. Stir in the cilantro and white pepper.

With damp hands, form a portion of the shrimp mixture around the end of a sugarcane piece, so that the mixture covers about two-thirds of the stick. Place on a lightly greased baking tray and repeat with the remaining shrimp mixture and sugarcane pieces. Cover and refrigerate for 30 minutes.

Preheat a grill to high and lightly grease with oil.

Meanwhile, to make the nuoc cham, combine the sugar, vinegar, fish sauce, and ½ cup water in a small saucepan over medium–low heat. Bring to a gentle simmer and stir until the sugar has dissolved. Remove from the heat and set aside to cool slightly. Mix in the lime juice, garlic, and chili. Set aside to cool to room temperature.

Cook the sugarcane shrimp for about 5 minutes, turning occasionally, until golden all over. Serve hot with the dipping sauce alongside.

PROSCIUTTO-WRAPPED SCALLOPS

SERVES 4

12 large scallops, cleaned

olive oil, for drizzling

juice of 1 lemon

2 thyme sprigs, leaves picked

salt and freshly ground black pepper

6 slices prosciutto, cut in half
  lengthways

4 bamboo skewers, soaked in
  cold water

Preheat a griddle to high and lightly grease with oil.

Drizzle the scallops lightly with olive oil and sprinkle with the lemon juice and thyme. Season with salt and pepper.

Wrap each scallop carefully with a slice of prosciutto and thread onto the bamboo skewers.

Cook for 1½ minutes on each side and serve immediately.

LOBSTER TAIL & SALAD SLIDERS

MAKES 8 SLIDERS

3 tablespoons butter, softened

3 tablespoons finely chopped
  flat-leaf parsley

zest of 1 lemon

pinch of sea salt flakes

2 lobster tails, halved lengthways

1 celery stalk, finely sliced

½ red apple, cored and finely sliced

1 tablespoon finely chopped dill

3 tablespoons whole egg mayonnaise

3 tablespoons crème fraîche

1 butter lettuce, leaves separated

8 slider buns, halved and toasted

Preheat grill to high and lightly grease with oil.

Combine the butter, parsley, lemon zest, and salt in a bowl.

Place the lobster tail halves, cut-side down, on the grill and cook for 2–3 minutes until slightly charred. Turn and spread the lobster tails with the seasoned butter. Continue grilling for a further 3–5 minutes until the lobster meat is tender. Remove from the heat, cover loosely and set aside to cool.

Toss the celery, apple, and dill together in a bowl. Add the mayonnaise and crème fraîche and mix well.

Remove the lobster meat from the shells and chop into ½ in discs. Stir gently into the salad, coating well with the dressing.

Place the lettuce leaves onto the bun bases, and divide the salad equally between the 8 buns. Top with the lids and secure with toothpicks. Serve immediately.

CRISPY SKIN SALMON WITH FENNEL & CELERY REMOULADE

SERVES 4

4 × 7 oz skin-on salmon fillets
lemon cheeks, to serve

FENNEL & CELERY REMOULADE

¼ cup whole egg mayonnaise
¼ cup Greek-style yogurt
1 teaspoon dijon mustard
1 tablespoon finely chopped
  flat-leaf parsley
1 tablespoon finely chopped chives
2 teaspoons finely chopped tarragon
1 tablespoon roughly chopped
  capers
2 cornichons, finely chopped
2 fennel bulbs, halved lengthways,
  cored and shaved
2 celery stalks, thinly sliced
  on the diagonal

To make the remoulade, combine the mayonnaise, yogurt, and mustard in a large mixing bowl. Add the parsley, chives, tarragon, capers, and cornichons and stir thoroughly. Mix in the fennel and celery and season with black pepper to taste. Cover with plastic wrap and refrigerate until required.

Preheat a griddle to high and lightly grease with oil.

Pat the salmon skin dry with paper towel and sprinkle generously with salt. Cover and allow to rest for 20 minutes to bring to room temperature. The salt will cause the salmon skin to release moisture so pat dry again and sprinkle with a little more salt before cooking.

Cook the salmon skin-side down for 4 minutes or until crisp and golden. Turn the fillets and cook for another 1–2 minutes, depending on the thickness of the fillets, until medium rare.

Serve the salmon with the remoulade and lemon cheeks.

LAMB

MOROCCAN LAMB MEATBALLS WITH MINTED YOGURT

SERVES 4–6

Unleavened grilled flatbread
   (page 135), to serve
½ red onion, finely sliced
chopped mint, to serve
chopped flat-leaf parsley, to serve
cherry tomatoes, halved, to serve

MOROCCAN MEATBALLS

1 tablespoon ground cumin
1 tablespoon sweet paprika
4 garlic cloves, finely chopped
1 teaspoon sea salt flakes
½ cup cilantro leaves, chopped
juice of ½ lemon
1 egg
3 tablespoons olive oil
3 tablespoons pine nuts, lightly
   toasted and roughly chopped
2 lb 3 oz ground lamb

MINTED YOGURT

1 cup natural yogurt
pinch of sugar
1 tablespoon finely chopped mint

To prepare the meatballs, combine the cumin, paprika, garlic, salt, cilantro, lemon juice, egg, olive oil, and pine nuts in a large mixing bowl. Add the lamb and mix well using your hands. Using wet hands, roll the mixture into golf ball-sized balls and flatten slightly into thick patties. Place on a tray, cover with plastic wrap and refrigerate for 1 hour.

Preheat a griddle to medium and lightly grease with oil.

To make the minted yogurt, combine the ingredients in a bowl.

Cook the meatballs, turning occasionally, for about 7–8 minutes until cooked through.

Toast the flatbreads on one side only for 20 seconds until warmed through and a little charred in places.

Serve by loading each uncharred side of the flatbread with onion, mint, parsley, tomato, a few meatballs, and then drizzling with the minted yogurt.

GRILLED LAMB LOIN WITH ANCHOVY & GARLIC BUTTER

SERVES 4

3 tablespoons olive oil

½ teaspoon sea salt flakes

2 rosemary sprigs, roughly chopped

8 thick lamb loin chops

ANCHOVY & GARLIC BUTTER

6 anchovies, finely chopped

2 garlic cloves, crushed

3 tablespoons finely chopped
  flat-leaf parsley

zest of ½ lemon

4½ oz butter, softened

To make the butter, pound the anchovies, garlic, parsley, and lemon zest to a paste using a mortar and pestle. Combine with the butter and mix well. Lay a sheet of baking paper on a work surface and spoon the butter into a thick line in the center. Roll into a log and chill until needed.

In a small bowl, combine the oil, salt, and rosemary. Brush the lamb chops with the oil, cover with plastic wrap and set aside for 30 minutes to come to room temperature.

Preheat a grill to high and lightly grease with oil.

Cook the lamb chops for 3–4 minutes on each side for medium, or 4–5 minutes on each side for well done. Transfer to a plate, cover loosely with foil and rest for 5 minutes.

Slice the anchovy butter into discs and serve on the lamb chops.

SPICY KASHMIRI ROAST LAMB

SERVES 6

3½ lb butterflied boneless
  lamb leg
½ cup natural yogurt
½ cup almonds
1 tablespoon honey

KASHMIRI SPICE MIX

¾ in piece ginger, grated
4 garlic cloves, crushed
1 small red chili, finely chopped
1½ teaspoons sea salt flakes
1 teaspoon ground cumin
1 teaspoon ground turmeric
½ teaspoon ground cardamom
½ teaspoon freshly ground
  black pepper
juice of ½ lemon
3 tablespoons olive oil

Preheat a hooded grill to medium and lightly grease with oil.

To make the spice mix, combine the ingredients in a small bowl. Rub all over the lamb to coat well.

Blend the yogurt, almonds, and honey in a food processor until smooth. Coat the spiced lamb with the yogurt mixture.

Place the lamb on the grill and cook, covered, for about 40 minutes, turning once halfway through. Cooking times will vary; if lamb is still rare, turn again and cook for a further 10–15 minutes until cooked through. Remove from the heat, cover and rest for 15 minutes before slicing.

RACK OF LAMB WITH ROSEMARY CRUST

SERVES 4–6

---

2 racks of lamb, with 6–8 points on
 each rack
1 tablespoon olive oil, plus extra
 for brushing
2 garlic cloves, crushed
1 tablespoon wholegrain mustard
zest of 1 lemon
2 rosemary sprigs, finely chopped
3 tablespoons finely chopped
 flat-leaf parsley
1 tablespoon dry breadcrumbs

Cut the lamb racks in half, to make 4 racks of 3–4 cutlets each. Brush the racks with olive oil and season on both sides with salt and pepper.

In a small bowl, combine the olive oil with the garlic, mustard, and lemon zest. Place the lamb racks bone-side down on a tray and spread the mustard mixture evenly on the fat side.

Combine the rosemary, parsley, and breadcrumbs in a small bowl. Press the mixture firmly into the mustard to help it adhere. Set aside to rest for 30 minutes.

Preheat a hooded grill to medium-high heat and lightly grease with oil.

Cook the lamb racks, crust-side down, for 3 minutes, then turn and cook for another 6 minutes. Lower the heat to medium. Stand the racks upright, leaning against each other to balance, then cover the barbecue and cook for 15–20 minutes or until done to your liking.

Remove the lamb from the heat, cover loosely with foil and rest for 10 minutes before slicing into cutlets to serve.

GREEK-STYLE SLOW-COOKED LAMB ROAST

SERVES 6

4 rosemary sprigs

4 mint sprigs

8 oregano sprigs

1 small bunch thyme

4 lemon balm sprigs

1 lemon, sliced

6 garlic cloves, unpeeled

5½ lb lamb leg

3 tablespoons olive oil

1 teaspoon sea salt flakes

½ teaspoon freshly ground
   black pepper

green salad and Summer veg
   ratatouille parcels (page 132),
   to serve (optional)

Preheat a hooded grill to low and lightly grease with oil.

Line a baking tin with baking paper and spread half the herbs, lemon slices, and garlic over the bottom.

Rub the lamb leg with the olive oil, salt, and pepper, and place it on top of the herbs. Put the remaining herbs, lemon, and garlic on and around the lamb.

Place the baking tin on the grill, cover and cook for up to 5 hours, until the lamb is caramelized and tender (cooking time will depend on the barbecue heat and the size of the roast). After cooking for 3 hours, check for doneness every 30 minutes, replacing the cover and continuing to cook if required.

Remove from the heat, cover in foil and rest for 20 minutes before carving.

This roast is great served with a simple green salad and Summer veg ratatouille parcels.

MINT & GARLIC LAMB KEBABS WITH QUINOA TABBOULEH

MAKES 10 SKEWERS

2½ lb boneless lamb leg, cut into
   2 in cubes
10 tiny onions (pickling onions),
   peeled and halved
2 zucchini, cut into ¾ in rounds
Yeasted or Unleavened grilled
   flatbread (pages 134–135), to serve
   (optional)
Roasted chickpea & garlic hummus,
   (page 149), to serve (optional)

MARINADE

1 cup natural yogurt
3 tablespoons extra-virgin olive oil
2 garlic cloves, roughly chopped
zest and juice of 1 lemon
½ cup mint leaves
¼ cup flat-leaf parsley leaves
1 tablespoon sea salt flakes
1 teaspoon freshly ground black
   pepper

QUINOA TABBOULEH

½ cup red quinoa, well rinsed
1½ cups flat-leaf parsley leaves,
   finely chopped
1 cup mint leaves, finely sliced
1 tablespoon chopped oregano
4 scallions, very finely sliced
3 plum tomatoes, diced
⅓ cup lemon juice
⅓ cup extra-virgin olive oil

To make the marinade, blend the ingredients until smooth using a blender or food processor.

Place the lamb in a large zip-lock bag and pour in the marinade. Seal the bag, pushing out as much air as possible. Massage the bag to ensure the lamb is well coated in the marinade. Refrigerate for 4–8 hours.

To make the tabbouleh, bring a small saucepan of water to the boil and cook the quinoa over medium–low heat for 15 minutes or until tender. Drain and set aside to cool. Combine the quinoa, parsley, mint, oregano, scallions, and tomatoes in a large serving bowl. Whisk together the lemon juice and olive oil and season to taste. Pour over the quinoa mixture and toss well.

Preheat a grill to medium–high and lightly grease with oil.

Thread cubes of marinated lamb onto 10 flat metal skewers, alternating with pieces of onion and zucchini.

Cook the kebabs for about 8–12 minutes, turning, until browned all over and cooked through.

Transfer the kebabs to a platter and rest for 5 minutes. If desired, serve with Grilled flatbread and Roasted chickpea & garlic hummus.

TANDOORI-STYLE LAMB CHOPS

SERVES 6

12 lamb chops
lemon or lime wedges, to serve

TANDOORI MARINADE

2 teaspoons chili powder
1 teaspoon ground cumin
1 teaspoon ground coriander
1 teaspoon ground turmeric
½–1 teaspoon salt
3 tablespoons vegetable or canola oil
3 tablespoons white vinegar
½ cup Greek-style yogurt

To make the marinade, combine the ingredients in a dish that will comfortably fit the chops. Add the chops to the marinade and mix to coat well. Cover and refrigerate for at least 1 hour.

Preheat a grill to high and lightly grease with oil.

Cook the chops for 2–3 minutes on each side for medium, or 3–4 minutes on each side for well done. Transfer to a plate, cover loosely with foil and rest for 2 minutes.

Serve with lemon or lime wedges for squeezing over.

LAMB CHOPS WITH PRESERVED LEMON GREMOLATA SERVES 6

¼ cup white vinegar

2 teaspoons salt

½ teaspoon freshly ground black pepper

1 teaspoon dried oregano

2 garlic cloves, crushed

3 tablespoons olive oil

6 lamb chump or shoulder chops

PRESERVED LEMON GREMOLATA

¼ preserved lemon, skin only, finely diced

1 small handful parsley, finely chopped

½ garlic clove, crushed

Combine the vinegar, salt, pepper, oregano, garlic, and olive oil in a large dish that will comfortably fit the chops. Add the chops to the marinade and mix to coat well. Cover and refrigerate for at least 2 hours.

Preheat a grill to high and lightly grease with oil.

Cook the chops for 3 minutes on each side for medium, or 4 minutes on each side for well done. Transfer to a plate, cover loosely with foil and rest for 3 minutes.

Meanwhile, for the gremolata, combine the ingredients in a small bowl.

Serve the chops sprinkled with the gremolata.

CHERMOULA LAMB SHOULDER WITH GARLIC & TAHINI YOGURT

SERVES 4–6

2½ lb butterflied boneless lamb shoulder
chopped cilantro leaves, to serve
chopped flat-leaf parsley, to serve

CHERMOULA

2 teaspoons cumin seeds
2 teaspoons coriander seeds
1 small onion, roughly chopped
3 garlic cloves, crushed
¾ in piece ginger, finely grated
zest and juice of 1 lemon
1 cup cilantro leaves, roughly chopped
1 cup flat-leaf parsley leaves, roughly chopped
1 teaspoon smoked paprika
1 teaspoon salt
½ cup extra-virgin olive oil

GARLIC & TAHINI YOGURT

½ cup Greek-style yogurt
juice of ½ lemon
1 tablespoon tahini
1 small garlic clove, crushed
¼ teaspoon ground cumin
sea salt flakes

To make the chermoula, toast the cumin and coriander seeds in a small dry frying pan over medium heat for about 2 minutes until fragrant. Transfer to a food processor along with the remaining ingredients. Process until well combined.

Rub the chermoula all over the lamb shoulder, cover with plastic wrap and refrigerate for 2 hours or overnight.

Remove the lamb from the fridge 1 hour before cooking.

Preheat a hooded grill to medium–high and lightly grease with oil.

Cook the lamb skin-side down for 15 minutes. Turn and cook for a further 10 minutes. Reduce the heat to medium, cover and cook for a further 15–18 minutes. Remove from the heat, cover with foil and rest for 10 minutes.

To make the yogurt sauce, combine the ingredients in a small bowl.

Slice the lamb thinly, drizzle with the sauce and garnish with the herbs to serve.

BEEF

GRILLED STEAK WITH BÉARNAISE SAUCE

SERVES 4

4 New York strip or top sirloin steaks
Chargrilled Belgian endive (page
 143), to serve (optional)
1 tablespoon olive oil

BÉARNAISE SAUCE

9 oz butter
2 shallots, finely chopped
3 tablespoons white wine vinegar
2 large egg yolks
1 tablespoon lemon juice, plus extra
 if required
1 tablespoon finely chopped tarragon

To make the béarnaise sauce, heat 1 tablespoon of the butter in a small saucepan over medium heat. Add the shallots and a grind of black pepper and cook for 30 seconds. Add the vinegar, reduce the heat to medium–low, and cook for 2–3 minutes until the vinegar has evaporated. Reduce the heat to low and continue cooking for about 5 minutes until the shallots are tender and translucent. Transfer to a small bowl to cool.

Heat the remaining butter in a small saucepan over medium heat for 2–3 minutes until it foams. Transfer to a small jug and keep hot.

Combine the vinegar reduction with the egg yolks, lemon juice, tarragon, and 1 tablespoon water in a small food processor and blend until smooth. With the motor running, add the hot butter in a thin, steady stream, discarding the milk solids in the bottom of the jug. Continue blending for 2–3 minutes until a smooth, creamy sauce forms. Pour the sauce into a medium-sized bowl and season to taste with salt, pepper, and more lemon juice, if desired. Cover and keep warm. Béarnaise sauce can be served at room temperature, but it is very tricky to reheat if you let it go cold.

Brush the steaks with the oil and season both sides lightly with salt and pepper. Cover and set aside for 20 minutes to bring to room temperature.

Preheat a grill to high and lightly grease with oil.

When the grill is smoking hot, cook the steaks for 4 minutes on each side for medium rare (you can cook a little less or more according to your preference). Remove from the heat, cover and rest for 5 minutes.

Serve with the béarnaise sauce and, if desired, Chargrilled Belgian endive.

ARGENTINIAN BEEF WITH CHIMICHURRI

SERVES 6–8

4½ lb beef top sirloin cap (picanha), with fat cap intact

SPICE RUB

1 tablespoon smoked sweet paprika

1 tablespoon sea salt flakes

2 teaspoons ancho chili powder

1 teaspoon soft brown sugar

1 teaspoon freshly ground black pepper

CHIMICHURRI

2 cups flat-leaf parsley leaves, roughly chopped

1 cup cilantro leaves, roughly chopped

½ cup mint leaves, roughly chopped

3 garlic cloves, roughly chopped

2 shallots, roughly chopped

2 long red chilies, deseeded and roughly chopped

¼ cup lemon juice

3 tablespoons sherry vinegar or red wine vinegar

1 teaspoon sea salt flakes

½ teaspoon freshly ground black pepper

¾ cup extra-virgin olive oil

To make the spice rub, combine the ingredients in a small bowl.

Place the beef on a clean work surface and, using a sharp knife, score the fat in a crosshatch pattern. Cut deeply, but don't cut into the meat. (This will help to baste the meat as it cooks by evenly releasing the flavorsome fat, and it will also stop the sides of the meat from curling.) Massage the spice rub deeply into the grooves and all over the meat. Cover with plastic wrap and refrigerate for 2 hours.

To make the chimichurri, blend the parsley, cilantro, mint, garlic, shallots, chili, lemon juice, vinegar, salt, and pepper in a food processor until a coarse paste forms. With the motor running, add the oil in a thin, steady stream until incorporated. Taste and adjust the seasoning, then transfer to a small bowl, cover with plastic wrap and refrigerate until needed.

Preheat a hooded grill to high and lightly grease with oil.

Place the beef, fat-side up, on the grill, cover and reduce the heat to medium-low. Cook for 45 minutes. Turn the beef and cook for a further 15 minutes. Turn again and cook for another 10 minutes for medium. (You can cook a little less or more according to your preference.) Transfer to a plate, cover loosely with foil and rest for 20 minutes before slicing.

Slice the beef thickly and serve on a platter drizzled with half the chimichurri. Serve the remainder of the sauce in a small bowl for guests to help themselves.

THE BOSS BEEF BURGERS

SERVES 4

1 lb ground lean beef

1 red onion, finely chopped

½ cup flat-leaf parsley leaves, finely
chopped

¼ cup basil leaves, finely chopped

¼ cup semi-sundried tomatoes,
finely chopped

1 egg

½ teaspoon sea salt flakes

¼ teaspoon freshly ground black
pepper

¼ teaspoon sweet paprika

olive oil, for brushing

4 round bread rolls, halved

4 slices gruyère

ketchup, mustard, mayonnaise,
relish and/or chili sauce, to serve

iceberg lettuce leaves, to serve

2 pickles, sliced

1 large tomato, sliced

Combine the beef, onion, parsley, basil, sundried tomato, egg, salt, pepper, and paprika in a large bowl. Mix well by hand. Divide into four even portions and, with wet hands, press into flat patties slightly wider than the bread rolls. Transfer to a plate, cover with plastic wrap and rest in the fridge for 30 minutes. (The patties will keep in the fridge for a few hours, so they can be prepared ahead of time.)

Heat a grill or griddle to medium and lightly grease with oil.

Brush or spray the burgers lightly with olive oil. Cook, turning occasionally, for 10 minutes or until cooked through. When almost cooked, top each burger with a cheese slice to melt and then toast the rolls lightly on both sides.

Spread the base of each roll with your sauce/s of choice then top with lettuce, pickles, the burger, and tomato slices. Spread the top with any other sauce, as desired, and dig in.

VEAL CUTLETS WITH SAGE, CAPERS & LEMON

SERVES 4

2 anchovies, roughly chopped

2 garlic cloves, finely chopped

1 tablespoon olive oil

4 × 9 oz veal cutlets

2 lemons, halved

4½ oz butter, coarsely chopped

1 tablespoon capers, drained

20 sage leaves

3 tablespoons lemon juice

In a small bowl, mash the anchovies with a fork. Stir in the garlic and olive oil. Brush the cutlets on both sides with the anchovy mixture, cover and set aside for 30 minutes.

Preheat a grill to high and lightly grease with oil.

Cook the cutlets for 5 minutes on each side or until caramelized on the outside. Cook the lemon halves, cut-side down, for 3–4 minutes until beginning to char. Remove the veal and lemons from the heat, cover and rest for 5 minutes.

Reduce the heat to medium and place a small frying pan on the grill. Add the butter, and cook, swirling the pan to melt evenly, until the butter begins to foam. Add the capers and sage and cook until crisp. Mix in the lemon juice and remove from the heat.

Serve the cutlets topped with the sage, caper and lemon butter, and with the charred lemon halves for squeezing over.

SIRLOIN STEAK WITH CILANTRO & JALAPEÑO BUTTER

SERVES 4

4 sirloin steaks, about 7 oz each

olive oil, for brushing

Mexican corn on the cob
(page 141), to serve (optional)

lime wedges, to serve

cilantro leaves, to serve

CILANTRO & JALAPEÑO BUTTER

⅓ cup butter, softened

2 small jalapeño chilies, deseeded
and finely chopped

¼ cup cilantro leaves, finely chopped

zest of ½ lime

½ teaspoon sea salt

To make the butter, combine the ingredients in a small bowl, mixing well with a fork. Lay a sheet of baking paper on a work surface and spoon the butter into a thick line in the center. Roll into a log and chill until needed.

Preheat a grill to high and lightly grease with oil.

Brush the steaks with olive oil and season lightly with salt on both sides.

When the grill is smoking hot, cook the steaks for 4 minutes on each side for medium rare (you can cook a little less or more according to your preference). Remove from the heat, cover and rest for 5 minutes.

Slice the butter into discs and serve on top of the steak, along with the lime wedges and cilantro. Great accompanied by Mexican corn on the cob.

STICKY BEEF SHORT RIBS WITH BOURBON-LACED BBQ SAUCE

SERVES 4

4½ lb beef short ribs, cut between bones into single ribs

Apple & cabbage slaw (page 142), to serve (optional)

SPICE RUB

1 tablespoon smoked paprika

2 teaspoons sea salt flakes

1 teaspoon freshly ground black pepper

3 garlic cloves, crushed

⅓ cup olive oil

BARBECUE SAUCE

3 tablespoons olive oil

1 onion, finely chopped

2 garlic cloves, crushed

1 long red chili, deseeded and finely chopped

⅓ cup cider vinegar

¼ cup soft brown sugar

⅔ cup pureed tomatoes

3 tablespoons lemon juice

⅓ cup pure maple syrup

2 teaspoons dijon mustard

3 tablespoons worcestershire sauce

⅓ cup bourbon

To make the spice rub, combine the ingredients in a small bowl. Coat the ribs with the rub, massaging the seasoning in well. Cover with plastic wrap and refrigerate for 2 hours.

Preheat the oven to 300°F.

Place the ribs in a baking tin in a single layer. Cook for 2–2½ hours until tender.

Meanwhile, to make the barbecue sauce, heat the oil in a medium-sized saucepan over medium–low heat. Cook the onion, stirring occasionally for 8–10 minutes until softened. Add the garlic and chili and cook for a further 4 minutes. Add the vinegar, sugar, pureed tomatoes, lemon juice, maple syrup, mustard, worcestershire sauce, and bourbon. Stir to combine and bring to the boil. Reduce the heat and simmer for about 15 minutes until it develops a thick pouring consistency. Season to taste and set aside to cool.

Preheat a grill to medium–high and lightly grease with oil.

Brush the ribs with barbecue sauce and cook on the grill, turning regularly and basting, for 20–30 minutes until a charred and sticky crust forms. Serve with the remaining barbecue sauce and, if desired, Apple & cabbage slaw.

THAI CHILI-COCONUT SURF & TURF SKEWERS

SERVES 4

24 large raw shrimp, peeled,
  with tails left intact
11 oz sirloin steak, thinly sliced
  across the grain
bamboo skewers, soaked in
  cold water
cucumber slices, to serve
mint leaves, to serve
lime wedges, to serve

CHILI-COCONUT MARINADE

1¼ cups coconut milk
2 lemongrass stalks, white part only,
  finely chopped
6 kaffir lime leaves, finely chopped
2 long red chilies, finely chopped
2 teaspoons grated palm sugar
zest and juice of 1 lime
2 tablespoons fish sauce
1 tablespoon kecap manis
2 tablespoons peanut oil

To make the marinade, combine the coconut milk, lemongrass, kaffir lime leaves, and chili in a small saucepan over low heat and simmer uncovered for 10 minutes. Set aside to cool to room temperature. Transfer to a food processor along with the palm sugar, lime zest and juice, fish sauce, and kecap manis. Process until well blended. With the motor running, add the oil in a thin, steady stream until incorporated.

Divide the marinade between two large bowls, adding the beef and shrimp to each separate bowl. Toss well to coat.

Thread the shrimp and beef onto separate skewers, threading the shrimp lengthways. Cover and refrigerate for 1 hour.

Preheat a grill to high and lightly grease with oil.

Cook skewers for 1–2 minutes each side or until just cooked through.

Serve with cucumber, mint leaves, and lime wedges.

GRILLED BEEF FAJITAS WITH SALSA & GUACAMOLE

SERVES 4–6

2½ lb beef skirt steak

2 red onions, halved and sliced

1 red bell pepper, sliced

1 green bell pepper, sliced

1 yellow bell pepper, sliced

10 flour tortillas

½ cup sour cream

6 oz queso fresco or feta, crumbled
(optional)

MARINADE

½ cup olive oil

3 garlic cloves, crushed

¼ cup soy sauce

juice of 2 limes

1 tablespoon soft brown sugar

1 tablespoon ground cumin

2 teaspoons ancho chili powder

2 teaspoons chili flakes

1 teaspoon sea salt flakes

½ teaspoon freshly ground
black pepper

FRESH TOMATO SALSA

1 long red chili, finely chopped

9 oz cherry tomatoes, roughly
chopped

1 cup cilantro leaves and stalks,
roughly chopped

juice of 1 lime

GUACAMOLE

1 avocado, peeled and diced

juice of ½ lime

To make the marinade, combine the ingredients in a small bowl and mix well.

Place the steaks in a dish and the onion and bell pepper in a second dish. Divide the marinade between the dishes and mix to coat. Cover with plastic wrap and refrigerate for 2 hours.

To make the salsa, combine the ingredients in a small bowl. Season to taste with salt and pepper. Cover and set aside until needed.

To make the guacamole, combine the ingredients in a bowl and mash roughly with a fork. Season to taste. Cover and set aside until needed.

Preheat a grill and griddle to high and lightly grease with oil.

Cook the steaks on the grill for 1–2 minutes, then turn. Cook for another 1–2 minutes, and turn again. Continue cooking, turning every minute or so, for 8–10 minutes in total, or until done to your liking. Transfer to a plate, cover loosely with foil and rest for 10 minutes.

Cook the bell pepper and onion mix on the griddle, turning occasionally, for 5–8 minutes or until just cooked and slightly charred. Transfer to a serving platter and keep warm.

Cut the steaks diagonally into thin slices and transfer to the serving platter.

Briefly toast the tortillas on one side over the hot grill and stack onto a board. Serve with the salsa, guacamole, sour cream, and cheese, if using, alongside.

VEGGIE

HALOUMI BURGERS WITH PEPERONATA **SERVES 4**

1 tablespoon olive oil

1¼ cups coarsely grated sweet
  potato

2 cups coarsely grated haloumi

5 oz zucchini, coarsely grated
  and squeezed to remove excess
  moisture

3 tablespoons finely chopped mint

3 tablespoons finely chopped
  Italian parsley

finely grated zest of 1 lemon

1 large egg

4 wholegrain burger buns, halved

1 large handful baby spinach
  or lettuce leaves

1 large tomato, sliced

PEPERONATA

3 tablespoons olive oil

2 garlic cloves, finely sliced

½ teaspoon dried chili flakes

1 small red onion, finely sliced

2 red bell peppers, sliced into
  ½ in strips

¼ teaspoon sea salt flakes

½ teaspoon soft brown sugar

Heat the olive oil in a small frying pan over medium heat. Fry the sweet potato for 4–5 minutes until cooked and just beginning to caramelize. Set aside to cool.

In a large mixing bowl, combine the haloumi, sweet potato, zucchini, mint, parsley, lemon zest, and egg.

Divide the mixture into four equal portions and, using wet hands, shape into patties. Cover with plastic wrap and refrigerate for at least 30 minutes to firm.

To make the peperonata, heat the olive oil in a medium-sized frying pan over medium heat. Add the garlic and chili flakes, and cook gently for 1 minute. Add the onion and bell pepper and cook, stirring frequently, for 15 minutes or until softened and beginning to caramelize. Add the salt and sugar and cook for a further 2 minutes.

Heat a griddle to medium and lightly grease with oil.

Brush or spray the burgers lightly with olive oil. Cook on the griddle for 3–4 minutes on each side until golden brown, using a metal spatula to gently turn the burgers.

Toast the burger buns lightly on each side, then assemble each with baby spinach or lettuce, tomato, a burger patty, and the peperonata.

GRILLED VEGETABLE & HALOUMI KEBABS

SERVES 4

7 oz haloumi, cut into ¾ in cubes

2 yellow bell peppers, cut into
   ¾ in chunks

2 zucchini, sliced into ½ in rounds

7 oz cherry tomatoes

2 red onions, cut into ¾ in chunks

bamboo skewers, soaked in
   cold water

salad leaves, to serve

lemon wedges, to serve

Yeasted grilled flatbreads (page 134),
   to serve (optional)

MARINADE

¼ cup olive oil

juice of 1 lemon

2 garlic cloves, crushed

1 red chili, finely chopped

8 mint leaves, finely chopped

1 tablespoon dried oregano

To make the marinade combine the ingredients in a large bowl and whisk well. Add the haloumi, bell peppers, zucchini, tomatoes, and onion, and toss to coat.

Preheat a griddle to medium and lightly grease with oil.

Thread the haloumi and vegetables onto the skewers. Cook the kebabs for 3–5 minutes on each side until the haloumi browns and the vegetables have slightly softened and caramelized.

Serve with salad leaves, lemon wedges, and flatbread (if desired).

POTATO FRITTERS WITH APPLE SAUCE

SERVES 4

1 lb potatoes, peeled and grated
2 small onions, grated
¼ teaspoon salt
½ cup all-purpose flour
2 eggs, lightly beaten
1 tablespoon vegetable oil

APPLE SAUCE

1 lb 3 oz granny smith apples, peeled,
  cored, and diced
¼ teaspoon ground cinnamon
pinch of salt
1 tablespoon sugar
squeeze of lemon juice

To make the apple sauce, place the ingredients and ⅓ cup water in a small saucepan over medium heat. Bring to the boil, then reduce the heat to low, cover and leave to cook for 15–20 minutes, until the apple has completely broken down. Remove from the heat and set aside to cool.
If you would like a smooth sauce, place in a blender and blend until smooth. For a chunkier sauce, just mash with a fork until the larger chunks have broken down.

Preheat a griddle to high and grease with oil.

Combine the potato, onion, salt, and flour in a bowl. Add the egg and oil and mix well. Fill a ⅓ measuring cup with the potato mixture and place the mixture on the griddle. Flatten until the fritter is about ½ in thick. Repeat this process, until you have 3–4 fritters on the griddle. Fry for 4–5 minutes on each side, until golden brown and cooked through. Transfer to paper towel to drain, then repeat with the remaining mixture.

Serve the fritters with warm or cold apple sauce on the side. Any leftover apple sauce will keep in an airtight container in the fridge for up to 1 week.

GRILLED SPICED CAULIFLOWER STEAKS

SERVES 4–6

---

2 large heads cauliflower, stalks trimmed

¼ cup olive oil

zest and juice of 2 limes

2 garlic cloves, crushed

3 tablespoons smoked paprika

1 teaspoon ground cumin

¼ teaspoon cayenne pepper

1 teaspoon salt

¼ cup finely chopped cilantro leaves

lime wedges, to serve

Preheat a hooded grill to high and lightly grease with oil.

Cut the cauliflower into thick steaks (you should get 4–6 steaks – reserve the offcuts for another use).

Whisk the olive oil, lime juice, and garlic together in a small bowl. In a separate bowl, combine the lime zest and the spices.

Brush one side of each cauliflower steak with the olive oil mixture and then sprinkle generously with the spice mixture. Place on the grill with the seasoned-side down. Brush the tops with the olive oil mixture and season with the spice mix. Cover and cook for 5–6 minutes. Turn the cauliflower and cook, covered, for another 5 minutes or until cooked through but still firm.

Serve sprinkled with chopped cilantro and with lime wedges alongside.

MIXED MUSHROOM QUESADILLAS

SERVES 4

3 tablespoons olive oil

2 shallots, finely sliced

3 garlic cloves, finely chopped

14 oz mixed mushrooms (such as portobello, brown, king, porcini, oyster, button, shimeji), sliced

2 jalapeño chilies, finely chopped

½ teaspoon sea salt flakes

¼ teaspoon freshly ground black pepper

8 soft corn tortillas, taco size

1 cup grated cheese such as queso fresco, mozzarella, fontina, cotija or parmesan

⅓ cup cilantro leaves, finely chopped, plus extra to garnish

Preheat a griddle to medium and lightly grease with oil.

In a large mixing bowl combine the olive oil, shallots, garlic, mushrooms, chilies, salt, and pepper.

Cook on the griddle, turning and stirring regularly, for 5–6 minutes, until the mushrooms and shallots become soft and begin to caramelize. Remove from the heat and set aside to cool slightly.

Top four tortillas with the mushroom mixture. Scatter the cheese and cilantro over and top each with a second tortilla. Place on the griddle and cook on both sides until golden brown and the cheese has melted.

Slice each quesadilla into quarters, garnish with cilantro and serve.

Note: Quesadillas can be made from 1 tortilla folded in half to make a half moon, or 2 tortillas filled to make a circle as described above. The half-moon shapes are great for kids as the fold reduces spillage.

JAPANESE OKONOMIYAKI

MAKES 8

1 cup all-purpose flour

⅓ cup corn starch

¼ teaspoon salt

¼ teaspoon sugar

¼ teaspoon baking powder

¾ cup vegetable stock

4 eggs

¼ cup pickled red ginger, plus extra
   to garnish

½ medium white or savoy cabbage,
   finely sliced

Okonomi sauce (see note),
   to serve

Japanese mayonnaise, to serve

8 scallions, finely chopped

In a large bowl, combine the flour, corn starch, salt, sugar, and baking powder. Add the stock, whisk well and refrigerate the batter for 1 hour.

Preheat a hooded griddle to medium and lightly grease with oil.

Add the eggs and pickled ginger to the batter and mix well. Stir in the cabbage.

Pour ladles of batter onto the oiled griddle to make eight pancakes. Cover and cook for 5 minutes or until browned on the bottom. (The cover helps the thick pancake cook through to the center.) Turn, cover and cook for a further 5 minutes or until browned. Turn once more and cook, uncovered, for another 2 minutes.

To serve, drizzle with Okonomi sauce and Japanese mayo and garnish with scallions and pickled ginger.

Note: Okonomi sauce is available from Asian grocery stores. A quick substitute sauce can be made by blending ¼ cup tomato ketchup, 1 tablespoon worcestershire sauce, 1 tablespoon soy sauce and 2 teaspoons of sugar.

SOUTHERN-STYLE GRILLED TOFU

SERVES 4

2 blocks (1½ lb total) extra-firm
  tofu, cut into quarters then drained
  and dried
Apple & cabbage slaw (page 142),
  to serve (optional)

DRY RUB
1 teaspoon ground coriander
1 teaspoon ground cumin
2 teaspoons dried oregano
2 teaspoons sweet paprika
1 teaspoon smoked paprika
1 teaspoon garlic powder
1 teaspoon soft brown sugar
1 teaspoon ground cinnamon
2 teaspoons sea salt
1 teaspoon freshly ground
  black pepper

Preheat a grill to high and lightly grease with oil.

To make the rub, combine the ingredients in a small bowl.

Coat the tofu on all sides with the rub. Cook for about 4 minutes or until
golden brown. Turn and cook for a further 4 minutes.

Remove from the heat and, if you like, serve with a side of Apple
& cabbage slaw.

HUMMUS & ZA'ATAR GRILLED VEGETABLE WRAPS

SERVES 4

2 red bell peppers, cut into 2 in
   pieces
2 zucchini, sliced lengthways into
   ½ in strips
2 eggplants, sliced into ½ in rounds
1 red onion, sliced into rings
4 large flatbread wraps
Roast chickpea and garlic hummus
   (page 149), to serve
2 cups baby spinach leaves
¼ cup mint leaves

ZA'ATAR MARINADE

1 tablespoon dried thyme
1 tablespoon sesame seeds
2 teaspoons sumac
½ teaspoon salt
¼ cup olive oil
juice of ½ lemon

Preheat a grill and griddle to medium and lightly grease with oil.

To make the za'atar marinade, combine the ingredients in a large bowl and whisk well.

Brush the bell pepper, zucchini, and eggplant with the marinade then place on the grill. Cook, turning once, for 4–6 minutes. Toss the onion in the remaining marinade and cook on the griddle for 8–10 minutes until tender and beginning to caramelize.

Toast the wraps on the grill briefly to soften.

Assemble the wraps by spreading each with a heaped tablespoon of hummus, and topping with a handful of spinach leaves, and the bell pepper, zucchini, eggplant, onion, and mint leaves before rolling up to serve.

KOREAN BULGOGI TOFU

SERVES 4

1½ lb firm tofu, drained and cut
  into cubes
½ onion, finely sliced
4 scallions, finely sliced
12 iceberg lettuce leaves
2 cucumbers, cut into short spears
3 tablespoons sesame seeds, toasted

MARINADE
¾ cup tamari
½ onion, finely chopped
½ nashi pear, cored and grated
2 garlic cloves, crushed
1 teaspoon grated ginger
3 tablespoons soft brown sugar
1 teaspoon chili flakes
½ teaspoon freshly ground
  black pepper
1 tablespoon sesame oil

To make the marinade, combine the ingredients in a small bowl.

Pour a little bit of marinade into the base of a dish, add the tofu, and pour the remaining marinade over. Cover and refrigerate for 20 minutes.

Preheat a griddle to medium and lightly grease with oil.

Cook the onion, scallions, and tofu, turning the tofu after 4–5 minutes and continue cooking until caramelized.

Serve the tofu cubes in lettuce leaves with cucumber spears and sprinkled with sesame seeds.

GRILLED MEDITERRANEAN PIZZA WITH BASIL OIL & RICOTTA

SERVES 4

2 zucchini, cut diagonally into
  ½ in slices
1 yellow bell pepper, cut into strips
1 red bell pepper, cut into strips
½ green bell pepper, cut into strips
½ red onion, sliced into wedges
5 field mushrooms, sliced
7 oz ricotta
½ cup grated parmesan

PIZZA DOUGH

¾ cup warm water
½ teaspoon active dried yeast
2⅓ cups strong flour
½ teaspoon sea salt flakes
¼ cup olive oil, plus extra
  for coating

BASIL OIL

¼ cup extra-virgin olive oil
½ cup basil leaves
2 garlic cloves, thinly sliced

To make the pizza dough, place the water in a small bowl and sprinkle the yeast over. Set aside for a few minutes until frothy. Combine the flour and salt in the bowl of an electric mixer fitted with a paddle attachment. Turn on to low speed and drizzle in the olive oil until combined. Slowly pour in the yeast mixture and mix until a sticky dough forms. Form the dough into a ball, cover with a little olive oil and place in a lightly oiled mixing bowl. Cover with plastic wrap and set aside in a warm place for 1–2 hours until the dough has doubled in size.

To make the basil oil, heat the oil in a small saucepan over medium–low heat. Add the basil leaves and garlic and swirl the pan until the leaves are wilted and the oil has become fragrant and turned a rich green color.

Preheat a hooded grill to high and lightly grease with oil.

Brush the zucchini, bell peppers, onion, and mushrooms with half the basil oil. Grill, turning occasionally, until the vegetables are tender and have defined grill marks. Set aside.

In a small mixing bowl, mash the ricotta and parmesan together with a fork.

Lightly grease a 16 in x 11 in rectangular baking tray or two round pizza trays. On a floured surface, roll out the pizza dough to fit the tray or trays. Brush the remaining basil oil over the base, adding the basil leaves and garlic. Scatter spoonfuls of the cheese over the base, and arrange the zucchini, bell peppers, onion, and mushroom over the top.

Place the tray or trays over the grill and close the lid. Cook for 10–15 minutes until the crust is golden brown.

EDAMAME BURGERS WITH RED ONION JELLY

MAKES 6 REGULAR OR 10 MINI BURGERS

6 full-sized or 10 mini sourdough
  rolls, halved

lettuce leaves, to serve

3 tomatoes, sliced

2 short cucumbers, sliced

RED ONION JELLY

¼ cup olive oil

1 lb red onions, thinly sliced

2 thyme sprigs

1 bay leaf

1 long red chili, thinly sliced

2 tablespoons soft brown sugar

1 teaspoon sea salt flakes

¼ teaspoon freshly ground black
  pepper

2 tablespoons balsamic vinegar

EDAMAME PATTIES

½ cup cashews

½ cup grated carrot

1 small onion, diced

2 garlic cloves, roughly chopped

½ cup flat-leaf parsley leaves,
  chopped

1 tablespoon tamari

2 cups podded edamame beans

1 cup chickpea flour

To make the red onion jelly, heat the oil in a medium-sized saucepan over medium heat. Add the onion, thyme, bay leaf, and chili. Cook, stirring regularly, for 25–30 minutes until softened and golden. Add the sugar, salt, pepper, vinegar, and ½ cup water. Bring to the boil then reduce the heat to low. Simmer, uncovered, for 8–10 minutes until thick and jammy.

To make the patties, blend the cashews, carrot, onion, garlic, parsley, tamari, and half the edamame beans in a food processor until it forms a chunky paste. Transfer to a large bowl. Add the remaining beans and the chickpea flour, season to taste and mix well. Cover with plastic wrap and refrigerate for 30 minutes (this will make it easier to handle when forming the patties).

Preheat a griddle to medium and lightly grease with oil.

Form the edamame mix into 6 or 10 patties and cook for 4–5 minutes each side until golden.

Place the lettuce and patties on the rolls and top with tomato, cucumber, and red onion jelly.

SIDES & SALADS

SUMMER VEG RATATOUILLE PARCELS

SERVES 4–6 AS A SIDE

2 red onions, halved and thickly sliced

4 garlic cloves, unpeeled

1 eggplant, sliced into ½ in rounds

2 zucchini, cut lengthways into ½ in strips

2 red bell peppers, halved and cut into strips

⅓ cup extra-virgin olive oil

½ teaspoon sea salt flakes

½ teaspoon freshly ground black pepper

4 thyme sprigs, leaves removed

1 lb tomatoes, deseeded and diced

2 teaspoons balsamic vinegar

basil leaves, to garnish

Preheat a grill and griddle to medium and lightly grease with oil.

In two separate bowls, toss the onion and garlic, and the eggplant, zucchini, and bell pepper in the olive oil.

Cook the onion and garlic on the griddle, and the eggplant, zucchini, and bell pepper on the grill. Cook for 6–8 minutes, turning occasionally, until softened and caramelized.

Transfer to a mixing bowl along with the salt, pepper, thyme, tomatoes, and balsamic vinegar. Toss to combine well.

Tear four 3 ft sheets of foil, and fold in half to make a double layer. Cut sheets of baking paper slightly smaller than the foil to place on top.

Use a slotted spoon to divide the vegetables evenly between the four sheets, placing the vegetables into the center of each. Lift the sides up and seal along the side edges by folding over twice (about ¾ in for each fold), leaving the tops open.

Divide the remaining juices from the bowl between the parcels, then fold the tops to seal, folding twice as before, but ensuring you leave some room for steam.

Reduce the grill heat to low and cook the parcels on the grill for 20 minutes.

Vegetable parcels can be served hot or at room temperature, garnished with basil leaves. Be careful when opening the foil parcels as the steam inside will be very hot.

YEASTED GRILLED FLATBREAD MAKES 4

2 cups strong flour
1 teaspoon sea salt flakes
1½ teaspoons active dried yeast
1 tablespoon butter, softened
about 5 fl oz warm water

Place the flour, salt, and yeast in a large mixing bowl. Add the butter and two-thirds of the water and mix by hand until the mixture comes together. Mix in enough of the remaining water for a dough to form.

Tip onto a lightly floured surface and knead the dough for 7–8 minutes until smooth and silky. Return the dough to the mixing bowl, cover with a clean damp dish towel and set aside in a warm place for about 1 hour, until the dough has doubled in size.

Preheat a griddle to medium-high and lightly grease with oil.

Flour your surface again. Tip the dough onto the surface and knock back to get the air out. Divide the dough into six portions and roll into balls. Roll out into ovals about ¼ in thick. Transfer to a lightly oiled baking tray and set aside for 10–15 minutes.

Place the flatbreads on the griddle and cook for about 3–4 minutes on each side until browned and blistered. Serve immediately.

UNLEAVENED GRILLED FLATBREAD MAKES 4

2 cups strong flour, plus extra if
  needed
¼ teaspoon ground cumin
¼ teaspoon ground coriander
¾ teaspoon sea salt flakes
3 tablespoons melted butter
1¾ cups warm milk

In a large bowl, combine the flour, cumin, coriander, salt, butter, and milk until a dough forms.

Tip onto a lightly floured surface and knead the dough for a few minutes until smooth. If the dough is too sticky, add a little extra flour. Wrap with plastic wrap and rest at room temperature for 30 minutes.

Preheat a griddle to medium-high and lightly grease with oil.

Flour your surface again. Divide the dough into four portions and roll into balls. Roll out into rounds about ¼ in thick.

Place the flatbreads on the griddle and cook for about 1 minute on each side, turning when the dough begins to bubble. Serve immediately.

GRILLED POTATO WEDGES WITH LIME YOGURT

SERVES 4 AS A SIDE

4 large floury potatoes, cut into
   wedges about 1¼ in thick
⅓ cup olive oil

SEASONING

1 teaspoon sweet paprika
1 teaspoon ancho chili powder
1 teaspoon sea salt flakes
½ teaspoon soft brown sugar

LIME YOGURT

¾ cup Greek-style yogurt
zest of ½ lime
2 teaspoons chopped cilantro leaves

Preheat a grill to medium–high and lightly grease with oil.

To make the seasoning, combine the ingredients in a small bowl.

Bring a large saucepan of salted water to the boil over high heat. Boil the
potato wedges for 5 minutes. Drain well.

To make the lime yogurt, mix the yogurt, lime zest, and cilantro in
a small bowl.

Brush the wedges with olive oil and place on the grill. Cook for 5-6 minutes
on each side until browned and crispy on the outside and tender inside.

Transfer the potatoes to a large bowl. Sprinkle with the spice mixture and
toss to coat. Serve immediately with lime yogurt alongside for dipping.

HERBY NEW POTATO SALAD

SERVES 4 AS A SIDE

---

1 lb small new red potatoes

½ teaspoon dijon mustard

½ teaspoon sea salt flakes

¼ teaspoon freshly ground black
 pepper

¼ cup olive oil

1 small red onion, very finely diced

2 tablespoons chopped chives

1 tablespoon chopped flat-leaf
 parsley

Place the potatoes in a medium-sized saucepan over high heat and cover with cold water. Bring to the boil, then reduce the heat to medium–low and simmer for 10–15 minutes until tender when tested with a skewer (be careful not to overcook as the skins may split and the potatoes will become waterlogged). Drain and set aside to cool slightly.

In a small bowl, combine the mustard, salt, pepper, and olive oil.

Cut the potatoes into bite-sized pieces and place in a medium-sized bowl along with the onion. Pour the dressing over while the potatoes are still hot, and toss to combine.

Allow to cool. Stir the chives and parsley through before serving.

MEXICAN CORN ON THE COB

SERVES 4 AS A SIDE

4 corn cobs, husks and silks removed
smoked paprika, for sprinkling
¼ cup finely grated parmesan or
  manchego cheese
1 lime, quartered, to serve

CHIPOTLE MAYO

juice of 1 lime
1 tablespoon chipotle sauce
½ cup good-quality whole egg
  mayonnaise

Heat a grill to high and lightly grease with oil.

Blanch the corn in a large saucepan of boiling water for 1 minute, then drain.

To make the chipotle mayo, combine the ingredients in a small bowl, stirring to combine well.

Brush or spray the corn with olive oil and cook on the grill, turning occasionally, for about 10 minutes until charred. Transfer to a platter.

Spread a small spoonful of chipotle mayo over each cob. Sprinkle with smoked paprika and scatter over the cheese.

Serve with any remaining chipotle mayonnaise and with lime wedges for squeezing over.

APPLE & CABBAGE SLAW

SERVES 4 AS A SIDE

¼ small red cabbage, finely shredded

¼ small green cabbage, finely shredded

2 small granny smith apples, cored and cut into matchsticks

4 scallions, finely sliced

1 cup cilantro leaves, roughly chopped

DRESSING

3 tablespoons lime juice

1 tablespoon cider vinegar

2 teaspoons dijon mustard

½ teaspoon salt

3 tablespoons olive oil

Combine the cabbage, apple, scallions, and cilantro in a large bowl.

To make the dressing, combine the lime juice, vinegar, mustard, salt, and olive oil in a small bowl.

Pour the dressing over the salad and toss to combine well.

CHARGRILLED BELGIAN ENDIVE

SERVES 4 AS A SIDE

4 large Belgian endive, halved
   lengthways
olive oil, for drizzling
juice of 1 lemon
1 tablespoon finely chopped
   flat-leaf parsley

Preheat a grill to high and lightly grease with oil.

Brush the endive halves with oil and season lightly with salt and freshly ground black pepper.

Place the cut-side down for 2–3 minutes, then turn and cook on the other side for another 2 minutes.

To serve, drizzle with a little extra olive oil and the lemon juice, and sprinkle with parsley.

FRESH CORN, BACON, KALE & JALAPENO SALAD

SERVES 4

4 slices rindless bacon

2 corn cobs, husks and silks removed

olive oil, for brushing

6–8 curly kale leaves, stems removed and leaves shredded

9 oz mixed cherry tomatoes, halved

2 avocados, cut into thick slices

4 scallions, finely chopped

½ jalapeño chili, deseeded and thinly sliced

toasted pumpkin seeds, to serve

TANGY LIME DRESSING

1 large egg yolk

⅓ cup lime juice

1 cup cilantro leaves with some chopped stem

2 teaspoons honey

½ jalapeño chili, deseeded and thinly sliced

½ cup olive oil

¼ cup vegetable oil

Cook the bacon in a non-stick frying pan over medium–high heat for 6–8 minutes, turning occasionally until browned and crisp. Transfer to a chopping board and cut into pieces.

Meanwhile, preheat a grill to medium.

Brush the corn with a little oil and cook on all sides until just charred and the kernels are tender. Remove, cool and cut off the kernels.

Combine the kale, tomato, avocado, corn, scallions, and chili in a large salad bowl.

For the dressing, combine the egg yolk, lime juice, cilantro, honey, chili, and a pinch of salt in a small food processor and blend until the cilantro is finely chopped. Combine the oils in a jug. While the motor is running, pour in the oil in a slow steady stream until the mixture has thickened. Season with pepper. If the dressing is too thick, just add a small amount of warm water.

Lightly toss the salad ingredients with the dressing. Scatter the bacon pieces over and top with toasted pumpkin seeds.

PORTUGUESE SALAD

SERVES 6 AS A SIDE

3 green bell peppers
6 plum tomatoes
3 garlic cloves, unpeeled
pinch of sea salt flakes
pinch of dried chili flakes
¼ cup extra-virgin olive oil
3 tablespoons sherry vinegar
1 baby romaine lettuce, leaves
   separated
½ cup cilantro leaves

Preheat a grill to high and lightly grease with oil.

Place the bell peppers, tomatoes, and garlic cloves on the grill to cook, turning occasionally with tongs, until the skins are charred and blistered all over. Transfer to a bowl, cover with plastic wrap and set aside to cool.

Peel the skins from the bell pepper, tomatoes, and garlic. Remove and discard the bell pepper seeds and chop the tomatoes and bell peppers roughly.

Pound the garlic, salt, and chili flakes into a paste using a mortar and pestle. Combine with the olive oil and sherry vinegar to make a dressing.

Combine the bell pepper, tomato, lettuce, and cilantro in a salad bowl. Pour the dressing over and toss to combine.

GRILLED EGGPLANT WITH SAGE OIL

SERVES 4–6 AS A SIDE

12 sage leaves, finely chopped, plus extra to garnish

1 teaspoon sea salt flakes

3½ fl oz olive oil

2 eggplants, sliced lengthways

Combine the sage leaves, salt, and olive oil in a small bowl. Brush the slices of eggplant with the sage oil. Allow to stand for 1 hour.

Preheat a grill to medium and lightly grease with oil.

Grill the eggplant slices for 2–3 minutes on each side until soft, and grill marks appear. Garnish with sage leaves to serve.

Note: Look for eggplants that have glossy skins and fresh green stems.

ROASTED CHICKPEA & GARLIC HUMMUS

SERVES 6 AS A SIDE

7 oz dry chickpeas
4 garlic cloves, unpeeled
3 tablespoons olive oil
1 teaspoon sea salt flakes
3 tablespoons lemon juice
½ teaspoon ground cumin
½ cup tahini
za'atar (see page 123, but make
    without the olive oil and lemon
    juice), to garnish
extra-virgin olive oil, for drizzling

Soak the chickpeas overnight in 4 cups cold water. Rinse and drain well. Transfer the chickpeas to a large saucepan and cover with 6 cups water. Simmer gently, covered, for about 1½ hours or until very tender. Drain, reserving the cooking liquid. Rinse the chickpeas in water and drain again.

Preheat the oven to 350°F.

In a medium-sized bowl, combine the chickpeas, garlic cloves, and olive oil. Spread onto a baking tray lined with baking paper and bake for 20 minutes or until the chickpeas start to color. Remove from the oven and set aside to cool a little.

When cool enough to handle, squeeze the garlic from the skins. Place the garlic and chickpeas in a food processor along with the salt, lemon juice, cumin, tahini, and ⅔ cup of the reserved chickpea cooking liquid.

Pulse for a few minutes until creamy. Adjust the thickness if required by adding a little warm water. The hummus will thicken on standing. Transfer to a small serving bowl and sprinkle with za'atar and drizzle with extra-virgin olive oil.

GRILLED CAULIFLOWER & SWEET POTATO SALAD WITH TAHINI-YOGURT DRESSING

SERVES 4 AS A SIDE

1 cauliflower, cut into florets

1 lb sweet potato, peeled, cut into
¾ in pieces

1 large red onion, cut into thin wedges

2 garlic cloves, crushed

¾ in piece ginger, grated

1 long red chili, finely chopped

⅓ cup extra-virgin olive oil

14 oz tinned chickpeas, rinsed and
drained

⅔ cup cilantro leaves, chopped

SPICE MIX

2 teaspoons ground cumin

2 teaspoons ground coriander

1 teaspoon ground cinnamon

½ teaspoon ground allspice

TAHINI-YOGURT DRESSING

½ cup Greek-style yogurt

1 tablespoon tahini

1 garlic clove, crushed

1 tablespoon lemon juice

Preheat a griddle to medium and lightly grease with oil.

To make the spice mix, combine the ingredients in a small bowl.

In a large bowl, combine the cauliflower, sweet potato, onion, garlic, ginger, chili, and olive oil.

Cook the vegetable mix on the griddle, turning regularly, for 8–10 minutes until the sweet potato is cooked through. Return to the mixing bowl and set aside to cool.

To make the dressing, combine the ingredients in a bowl.

Add the chickpeas to the vegetables then sprinkle the spice mix and cilantro over the top. Stir through to combine well.

Pour the dressing over the salad just before serving and toss well to coat.

GRILLED BAKED POTATOES SERVES 4

4 whole washed potatoes or small sweet potatoes

Preheat a hooded grill to medium and grease with oil.

Poke a few deep holes in the potatoes with a metal skewer. Wrap each potato in two layers of foil, ensuring they are well covered.

Place the potatoes on the grill and cover. Cook for 30 minutes, then turn and cook for another 20–30 minutes, until the flesh is tender (test by inserting a metal skewer).

Remove the foil from the potato and cook, turning occasionally, for 10 minutes, or until browned all over.

Serve with any of the toppings opposite.

AVOCADO, FETA & DUKKAH

1 tablespoon almonds
1 tablespoon pistachio nuts
1 tablespoon pine nuts
2 teaspoons coriander seeds
2 teaspoons cumin seeds
1 tablespoon sesame seeds
½ teaspoon sea salt flakes
pinch of ground cinnamon
pinch of ground nutmeg
Grilled baked potatoes
  (see recipe left)
⅔ cup crumbled feta
1 avocado, roughly mashed

Toast the almonds and pistachios in a large frying pan over medium-high heat, stirring, for 5 minutes or until just starting to color and become fragrant. Set aside and add the pine nuts and coriander seeds to the hot pan. Toast and stir for a minute, then add the cumin and sesame seeds. Continue to toast, stirring, until golden brown.

Using a mortar and pestle, pound the nuts, toasted spices, salt, cinnamon, and nutmeg until coarsely ground.

Split the tops of the baked potatoes and fill with feta and avocado then sprinkle with the dukkah.

CHEESE & SCALLION COLESLAW

1 cup finely sliced red cabbage
1 cup finely sliced green cabbage
1 carrot, grated
1 tablespoon white vinegar
1 teaspoon superfine sugar
1 teaspoon sea salt flakes
¼ cup whole egg mayonnaise
4 scallions, finely chopped
Grilled baked potatoes
  (see recipe left)
1 cup grated aged cheddar

In a medium-sized mixing bowl, combine the cabbage and carrot. Sprinkle with the vinegar, sugar, and salt and toss to combine well. Set aside for 1 hour.

The cabbage will release liquid, so drain and squeeze out any excess moisture. Place the drained cabbage mixture into a clean mixing bowl along with the mayonnaise and scallions and stir to combine.

Split the tops of the potatoes and fill with cheddar. Place the potatoes back on the grill, close the hood and cook for 4–5 minutes until the cheese has melted. Top with the coleslaw to serve.

SMOKED TROUT & HORSERADISH CRÈME

7 oz crème fraîche or sour cream
2 teaspoons finely grated
  horseradish
3 tablespoons chopped chives
7 oz smoked trout, flaked
  into small chunks
Grilled baked sweet potatoes
  (see recipe left)
¼ red onion, finely chopped
lemon wedges, to serve

In a medium-sized bowl, combine the crème fraîche or sour cream, horseradish, and chives. Gently stir in the smoked trout.

Split the tops of the sweet potatoes and fill with the smoked trout mixture. Add a teaspoon of red onion to the top of each and serve with lemon wedges for squeezing over.

GERMAN POTATO SALAD

SERVES 6 AS A SIDE

3 eggs

1 teaspoon olive oil

7 oz bacon, cut into batons

2 lb new potatoes

3 chicken stock cubes

½ red onion, thinly sliced

15 cornichons, sliced lengthways

1 small bunch flat-leaf parsley,
  chopped

1 small bunch chives, chopped

DRESSING

½ cup olive oil

¼ cup white wine vinegar

3 tablespoons dijon mustard

pinch of sugar

In a small bowl, whisk together the ingredients for the dressing, season with salt and freshly ground black pepper and set aside.

Place the eggs in a small saucepan, cover with cold water and bring to the boil over high heat. Reduce to a rolling simmer and continue cooking for 6 minutes. Remove from the heat and place the eggs directly into iced water. Once cool, peel and cut in half.

Heat the olive oil in a frying pan over high heat and add the bacon. Cook until crisp, then remove with a slotted spoon and set aside to drain on paper towel.

Place the potatoes in a large saucepan, cover with water and bring to the boil. Add the stock cubes and cook for about 15 minutes, until the potatoes are tender. Drain, then halve or quarter the potatoes depending on their size. Transfer to a large bowl and allow to cool for a few minutes. Add the red onion, bacon, cornichons, herbs, and the dressing. Toss to combine until everything is evenly coated in the dressing, then add the eggs and gently combine. Serve warm.

Note: The potatoes should be warm when tossed with the other ingredients, so it's best to prepare everything else first.

CUCUMBER SALAD

SERVES 4–6 AS A SIDE

2 long cucumbers
1 teaspoon table salt
½ red onion, thinly sliced
1 small bunch dill, chopped

DRESSING

¼ cup white vinegar
pinch of sugar
1 teaspoon celery salt
7 oz sour cream

Peel one of the cucumbers, then slice both cucumbers as thinly as possible.

Place the cucumber in a bowl, then add the salt and toss to combine. Set aside for 30–60 minutes, then drain away the excess liquid, lightly squeezing the cucumber to release excess moisture. Transfer to a clean bowl, add the red onion and toss to combine.

To make the dressing, mix the vinegar, sugar, celery salt, and sour cream in a small bowl until well combined. Season with black pepper.

Pour the dressing over the cucumber and onion and sprinkle with the chopped dill.

Toss to combine until the ingredients are evenly coated, then season to taste and serve immediately.

MEXICAN QUINOA SALAD

SERVES 6 AS A SIDE

2 corn cobs, husks and silks removed

1½ cups red quinoa, rinsed thoroughly

9 oz grape tomatoes, halved

1 red bell pepper, diced

1 red onion, finely diced

1 jalapeño chili, very finely diced

14 oz tinned black beans, rinsed and drained

2 cups cilantro leaves, finely chopped

¼ cup pumpkin seeds

DRESSING

3 tablespoons olive oil

juice of 2 limes

½ teaspoon sea salt flakes

1 teaspoon smoked paprika

½ teaspoon ground cumin

Heat a grill to high and lightly grease with oil.

Blanch the corn cobs in a large saucepan of boiling water for 1 minute, then drain. Brush or spray the corn with olive oil and cook on the grill, turning occasionally, for about 10 minutes until charred. Set aside to cool then cut the kernels off the cobs.

Bring 3 cups water to the boil in a medium saucepan over high heat. Add the quinoa, cover and simmer for about 15 minutes until all the moisture has been absorbed. Remove from the heat and keep covered.

To make the dressing, combine the ingredients in a bowl and whisk well.

To assemble the salad, mix the quinoa, corn, tomatoes, bell pepper, onion, chili, and beans in a large bowl. Pour the dressing over, add the cilantro and toss to combine. Scatter over the pumpkin seeds.

Serve at room temperature.

TURKISH ROASTED TOMATO SALAD

SERVES 4–6 AS A SIDE

6 plum tomatoes

4 large long red sweet peppers (such as bullhorn or cubanelle)

2 red bell peppers, finely chopped

1 bunch flat-leaf parsley, leaves finely chopped

1 red onion, coarsely chopped

DRESSING

2 garlic cloves, finely chopped

½ teaspoon chili flakes

1 teaspoon sweet paprika

1 teaspoon sea salt flakes

1 tablespoon lemon juice

¼ cup extra-virgin olive oil

1 tablespoon pomegranate molasses

Preheat a grill to medium–high and lightly grease with oil.

Cook the tomatoes and sweet peppers over the grill, turning occasionally, for 6–8 minutes until the skins are blackened and blistering. Seal in a plastic container or zip-lock bag and set aside to cool. Remove and discard the skins, stems and seeds. (Don't rinse as it will wash away the delicious charred flavor.)

Finely chop the tomato and pepper flesh and transfer to a large mixing bowl. Add the bell pepper, parsley, and onion and mix to combine.

To make the dressing, combine the ingredients in a small bowl. Stir well to blend.

Pour the dressing over the salad and toss well. Cover and refrigerate for 1 hour to allow the flavors to develop.

Serve at room temperature.

HOMEMADE TOMATO KETCHUP

MAKES 5 CUPS

6½ lb tomatoes, roughly chopped

2 granny smith apples, cored and roughly chopped

1 onion, roughly chopped

1 cinnamon stick

2 garlic cloves, crushed

1 teaspoon freshly ground black pepper

1 teaspoon ground allspice

2⅔ cups superfine sugar

3 tablespoons sea salt flakes

1⅔ cups apple cider vinegar

Place all the ingredients in a large saucepan over low heat. Simmer for 2 hours, uncovered, stirring frequently, or until the sauce reduces and thickens to a saucy consistency.

Strain the mixture through a fine-meshed sieve into a large bowl, pressing down to extract the liquid. Discard the solids.

Pour the hot mixture into sterilized bottles and seal. Store in a cool, dark place until ready to use. Once opened, the sauce will keep for up to 1 month in the fridge.

GRILLED CABBAGE SALAD

SERVES 4 AS A SIDE

¼ cup grated palm sugar

¼ cup lime juice

3 tablespoons fish sauce

2 garlic cloves, crushed

½ green cabbage, cut into thin wedges

¼ red cabbage, cut into thin wedges

3 tablespoons peanut oil

2 red Asian shallots, finely diced

1 long red chili, thinly sliced

Preheat a griddle to medium and lightly grease with oil.

Combine the palm sugar, lime juice, fish sauce, and garlic in a small saucepan over low heat. Simmer for 3–4 minutes until the sugar has dissolved and the mixture has reduced by a third. Remove from the heat.

Brush the cabbage wedges with the peanut oil and cook on the griddle for 6–8 minutes on each side, allowing the edges to blacken slightly.

Transfer to a chopping board and remove the cores from the cabbage. Place the cabbage wedges in a serving bowl and pour the dressing over.

Garnish with the shallots and chili.

WHITE BEAN SALAD WITH FRESH HERBS

SERVES 4–6

1½ cups dried haricot, navy or lima beans
3 flat-leaf parsley sprigs
2 thyme sprigs
1 bay leaf
2 garlic cloves, unpeeled
3 tablespoons white wine vinegar
½ cup olive oil
1 small red onion, finely diced
1 cup whole mixed olives
2 small tomatoes, diced
⅓ cup finely chopped flat-leaf parsley
handful basil leaves, torn

Place the beans in a saucepan, cover with plenty of cold water and bring to the boil. Reduce the heat and simmer for 10 minutes, then turn off the heat and leave to soak for 2 hours.

Drain the beans and cover with fresh water. Prepare a bouquet garni by tying the parsley and thyme sprigs and bay leaf together with unwaxed kitchen string. Add it to the beans with the garlic cloves. Bring to the boil, reduce the heat and simmer for 1½–2 hours, until the beans are tender, and adding more water as required; dried beans vary greatly in cooking time, so keep an eye on them.

Drain the beans well, discard the bouquet garni and garlic, and place the beans in a mixing bowl. While the beans are still warm, add the vinegar, olive oil, and onion, season with sea salt and toss gently to combine. Leave to cool.

Stir the olives, tomato, parsley, and basil through. Serve at room temperature.

CELERIAC REMOULADE

SERVES 4–6

1 small celeriac, about 1 lb
1 teaspoon salt (optional)
2 teaspoons lemon juice (optional)
1 tablespoon roughly chopped herbs,
    such as flat-leaf parsley, chervil
    or chives

REMOULADE

¾ cup homemade or good-quality
    mayonnaise
2 tablespoons dijon mustard
2 tablespoons lemon juice or
    white wine vinegar
sea salt and white pepper, to taste

Peel the celeriac, then cut into long thin julienne strips, either by hand, or using a mandoline if you have one. Taste the celeriac: if it's slightly bitter, toss it in a large bowl with the salt and lemon juice, set aside for 30 minutes, then rinse and dry well with paper towel. Place the celeriac in a large bowl.

To make the remoulade, put the mayonnaise, mustard, and lemon juice in a small bowl. Season with sea salt and white pepper and whisk together. Add the remoulade to the celeriac strips and toss to combine well. Cover and refrigerate for 2–3 hours, or overnight, for the celeriac to soften slightly.

This salad will keep in an airtight container in the fridge for up to 3 days. Serve sprinkled with the herbs.

DESSERTS

GRILLED PINEAPPLE WITH CINNAMON SUGAR & MINT

SERVES 8

1 pineapple, peeled, cored, and cut
   lengthways into 8 wedges
8 bamboo skewers, soaked in
   cold water
1 tablespoon softened butter
¾ cup soft brown sugar
2 teaspoons ground cinnamon
pinch of sea salt flakes
mint leaves, roughly chopped,
   to serve

Thread the pineapple wedges onto the skewers.

Preheat a grill to medium and lightly grease with oil.

In a small saucepan, cook the butter and brown sugar over low heat, stirring until the butter has melted and the and the sugar has dissolved. Add the cinnamon and salt and mix well. Remove from the heat.

Brush the sugar syrup over the pineapple wedges and cook on the grill for 3–5 minutes on each side, until caramelized.

Serve hot on a platter scattered with mint leaves.

CHERRY & CHOCOLATE DESSERT PIZZA

SERVES 6

½ teaspoon active dried yeast

1 tablespoon superfine sugar

1 tablespoon softened butter

⅓ cup warm milk

½ cup warm water

2 cups strong flour

½ teaspoon sea salt flakes

¼ cup mascarpone cheese

2 teaspoons soft brown sugar

zest of ½ lemon

2 cups cherries, pitted

shaved dark chocolate, for topping

mint leaves, to garnish

In a large jug, combine the yeast, superfine sugar, butter, milk, and water and stir well. Set aside for a few minutes.

Place the flour and salt in a large mixing bowl and make a well in the center. Pour the yeast mixture into the well and, using a spatula, draw the flour over the liquid to incorporate, until a dough forms. Tip onto a lightly floured work surface and knead the dough for 8 minutes or until smooth.

Return the dough to the bowl and cover with a clean damp dish towel. Leave to rise in a warm place for 1 hour or until the dough has doubled in size.

Preheat a hooded grill to medium–high and lightly grease with oil.

Knead the dough again lightly to knock out the air. Roll out into a circle, about 10 in in diameter, and place on a lightly oiled pizza tray.

In a small bowl, combine the mascarpone, brown sugar, and lemon zest, then spread the mixture over the dough base. Arrange the cherries evenly over the top, lightly pressing into the dough.

Place the tray on the grill, cover and cook for 15–20 minutes until the base is well cooked.

Remove from the heat and scatter with chocolate and mint leaves. Slice and serve.

GRILLED PEACHES WITH MASCARPONE & CARAMEL SAUCE

SERVES 4

¼ cup whole hazelnuts

4 peaches, halved and stones removed

1 tablespoon softened butter

⅓ cup mascarpone cheese

CARAMEL SAUCE

¾ cup soft brown sugar

¾ cup heavy cream

zest of ½ lemon

Preheat grill to medium–low and lightly grease with oil.

Heat a frying pan over medium heat and toast the hazelnuts for 1–2 minutes until toasted and fragrant. Set aside to cool then roughly chop.

To make the caramel sauce, combine the sugar with ¼ cup water in a small saucepan over low heat, stirring until the sugar has dissolved. Use a wet pastry brush to brush down the side of the pan to dissolve any remaining sugar crystals. Bring to the boil and cook, stirring, for about 8 minutes until the mixture turns a light golden color. Remove from the heat immediately. Set aside to cool for a few minutes then stir in the cream and lemon zest. The mixture may foam a little. Stir until smooth.

Brush the cut sides of the peaches generously with butter and place, cut-side down, on the grill. Cook for 4–5 minutes until grill marks appear.

Remove from the heat and serve immediately topped with mascarpone, caramel sauce, and hazelnuts.

GRILLED PEARS WITH CINNAMON & HONEY CREME FRAICHE

SERVES 4

4 firm beurre bosc or Packham
   pears, cored, unpeeled
4 cinnamon sticks
½ cup honey
½ teaspoon ground cinnamon
4 oz crème fraîche, to serve
thyme leaves, to garnish

Preheat a hooded grill to medium-low and lightly grease with oil.

Place a cinnamon stick in the hollowed core of each pear.

Wrap the pears in a double layer of foil and place on the grill. Cover and cook for 30 minutes.

Combine the honey and cinnamon with ½ cup water in a small saucepan over low heat. Cook, stirring occasionally, for 5 minutes or until the syrup thickens slightly. Set aside to cool.

Unwrap the cooked pears and serve whole. Add a dollop of crème fraîche and spoon the cinnamon and honey syrup over the top. Garnish with thyme leaves.

GRILLED FIGS WITH ROSEMARY & POMEGRANATE RICOTTA

SERVES 4

¼ cup walnut halves

7 oz ricotta

1 tablespoon pomegranate molasses, plus extra to serve

1 tablespoon lemon juice

1 tablespoon soft brown sugar

1 tablespoon finely chopped rosemary, plus extra sprigs to garnish

8 fresh figs, halved lengthways

Preheat a grill to medium and lightly grease with oil.

Heat a small frying pan over medium heat and toast the walnuts for 1–2 minutes until fragrant. Set aside to cool, then roughly chop.

Whisk the ricotta and pomegranate molasses together in a medium-sized mixing bowl.

In a small bowl, combine the lemon juice, sugar, and rosemary. Stir to dissolve the sugar.

Brush the cut side of the figs with the lemon mixture, then place, cut-side down, on the grill. Cook for 3–4 minutes until grill lines appear and the figs are hot.

Arrange the figs on serving plates with the ricotta and walnuts. Garnish with rosemary sprigs, and drizzle with a little extra pomegranate molasses.

NECTARINES WITH CITRUS & KAFFIR LIME SYRUP

SERVES 4

4 ripe nectarines, halved and stones removed
1 tablespoon melted coconut oil
vanilla bean or coconut ice cream, to serve (optional)
mint leaves, to garnish

CITRUS & KAFFIR LIME SYRUP

1 cup superfine sugar
⅓ cup lime juice
¼ cup orange juice
1 tablespoon lemon juice
3 kaffir lime leaves, shredded
¼ cup mint leaves

To make the syrup, combine the sugar and the lime, orange, and lemon juices with ⅓ cup water in a medium-sized saucepan over medium heat. Simmer until thickened and slightly syrupy. Add the kaffir lime and mint leaves and remove from the heat. Set aside for 20 minutes for the flavors to infuse.

Preheat a grill to medium–high and lightly grease with oil.

Brush the nectarine halves with the coconut oil and grill for 3–5 minutes on each side until grill marks appear.

Strain the leaves from the syrup. If the syrup has become too thick (it needs to pour), reheat gently and stir in a tablespoon of water.

Serve the nectarines with a scoop of ice cream (if you like) and a drizzle of the syrup. Garnish with mint leaves.

RUM-SPIKED GRILLED BANANA BOATS

SERVES 4

4 bananas, unpeeled
⅓ cup dark chocolate chips
¼ cup shredded coconut, toasted
1 teaspoon ground cinnamon
3 tablespoons honey
3 tablespoons dark rum
vanilla bean ice cream, to serve
  (optional)

Preheat a hooded grill to medium and lightly grease with oil.

Using four pieces of heavy-duty foil, shape a support for each banana by scrunching the foil up around the sides of the bananas, so they won't tip over while cooking on the grill.

Combine the chocolate, coconut, cinnamon, honey, and rum in a small mixing bowl. Cut a slit into the bananas lengthways, leaving ¾ in intact at each end. Cut deeply, but not through the skin at the back. Divide the chocolate mixture between the bananas.

Place the bananas in their foil boats on the grill. Cover and cook for 4–5 minutes until the skins have blackened and the chocolate has melted.

If you like, serve the bananas with a scoop of ice cream.

INDEX

Published in 2022 by Smith Street Books

Naarm | Melbourne | Australia
smithstreetbooks.com

ISBN: 978-1-922417-60-2

Publisher: Paul McNally
Senior Commissioning Editor: Hannah Koelmeyer
Editor: Aisling Coughlan
Recipe development: Sue Herold, Caroline Griffiths and Aisling Coughlan
Design concept: Kate Barraclough
Design layout: Heather Menzies, Studio31 Graphics
Photographer & Stylist: Billy Law
Proofreader: Pamela Dunne

Printed & bound in China by C&C Offset Printing Co., Ltd.

Book 202

10 9 8 7 6 5 4 3 2